The Big Idea

Is Technology Making Us Sick?

The Big Idea

Ian Douglas

Is Technology Making Us Sick?

A primer for the 21st century

Over 180 illustrations

General Editor:
Matthew Taylor

Contents

Introduction

A

We are, uniquely, the ape that makes complex tools and uses them to solve its problems. We call those tools technology.

Everything from language to clothing, flint spearheads, coracles, fishing hooks, sails, wattle and daub, food salting, gunpowder, candles, paper, glass lenses, printing, the spinning jenny, steam locomotives, telegraphs, antibiotics, microchips, hypertext transfer protocol, DNA sequencing machines, lithium-ion batteries and 5G mobile phone masts are technology, and every bit of it came into use in order to ease some particular sticking point that we encountered. We value our tools very highly. The fact that they can come at a cost to our own well-being matters to us less, and does not dim our enthusiasm for them.

Technology has always made us sick.

Hunter-gatherers 10,000 years ago first experienced diphtheria, syphilis, influenza, salmonella, tuberculosis and leprosy when they domesticated animals. The invention of agriculture, the first defining moment in the evolution of our civilization, reduced average prehistoric life expectancies from the mid-twenties to mid-teens. Neolithic people were anaemic; osteoporotic; deficient in zinc, calcium, vitamins D, B12 and A; and smaller in stature than their ancestors. Their teeth grew crooked and crowded, and fell out earlier due to the new, softer, more sugary diet. However, they did not return to the old, healthier ways because they had fire, pots, fabric, stone tools and permanent shelters for themselves and their stored food surpluses. They may not even have identified their new way of life as the cause of their sickness. It was an unintended, unexpected and unexplained side effect.

Agriculture, cultivating plants and raising livestock, began in parts of what is now the Middle East and independently, a few thousand years later, in the valleys of the Wei and Yellow rivers, now in China.

A   Neolithic arrowheads from Saharan Africa, c. 4,000 BC. These tiny pieces of stone, 3 cm (1¹/₅ in.) long, are among the first markers of us as a technological species.
B   Rock art from Tassili n'Ajjer, also Saharan Africa, from c. 7,000 BC shows early animal husbandry.
C   Contemporary images from the same region showing the use of carts and animals in agriculture.

B

C

We have never changed the pattern.

The ancients were fully aware of the poisoning that was caused by using lead for pipes and wine vessels – Nicander of Colophon wrote about it in the 2nd century BC – but the new material, pliable and with a low melting point, was too useful to give up. It was not until the late 20th century (1970 in Europe and 1986 in the USA) that lead was banned by building codes, ending two millennia of kidney failure, birth defects, diarrhoea and early deaths. It is still used in China.

In the 19th century, cholera, tuberculosis, typhoid, typhus and smallpox swept through the towns and cities that emerged around the new machine-powered factories. Workers lived closer together, sharing water sources and breathing space in the specialized buildings – put up to house the technology, with only the needs of the technology in mind – and infection spread more easily.

Nicander of Colophon was a greek poet and physician who wrote about poison in his 630-line poem entitled *Alexipharmaca.*

Horse manure was a big problem in cities. In New York in 1900 there were 100,000 horses that together produced around 1.36 million kilograms (1,500 tons) of manure every day, which had to be swept up and disposed of.

The **Factory Act** (1833) mandated shorter hours for children and introduced compulsory schooling and basic safety standards.

A

Abb. 32 (Siehe Seite 137)

Abb. 5 (Siehe Seite 74)

Abb. 11 (Siehe Seite 96)

B

C

Cars saved people from a mountain of horse manure but instead urban lungs filled with lead, micro-particulates and carbon monoxide, sending asthma rates skywards and changing the climate.

In addition to physical sickness caused by arranging our lives around machines, the direct use of machinery has always caused injury. Even when it has been clear to everyone that harm is being done to the people who make and operate machines, our love affair with shiny new things has been too strong to put them aside.

A   19th-century illustrations of a man with pulmonary tuberculosis, a man with typhoid and a man with cholera vomiting black fluid.

B   Child workers were the norm in the 19th and early 20th century, as seen here, working hard in a basket factory in Evansville, Indiana.

C   Boys packing brooms in the same factory. As late as 1900 most children in the USA left school at age 12 or 13 to take up working life.

Industrial workers in the 19th century, especially children, were at risk of mutilation every day as they came into contact with powerful machinery with little or no guards against accidents. Loss of limbs, fingers and hair were especially common, and reports of workers being swept into the relentlessly grinding cogs and crushed were far from rare. The inspectorate set up in 1833 in England as part of the Factory Act helped little as it had only four inspectors for more than 3,000 mills and factories, increasing to 35 in 1868. Coverage of deaths and maimings in the popular press put pressure on Parliament, and legislation was passed throughout the century, culminating in mandatory financial compensation in 1897. Demand for the goods produced grew rapidly throughout this time.

A

Scrivener's palsy afflicted writers and clerks in the 19th century just as repetitive strain injury paralyses the data entry workers of today. Their hands spasmed and they lost the ability to grip their pens. Some blamed the new steel nibs the clerks were using, whereas British anatomist Charles Bell (1774–1842) suggested the condition was due to 'the imperfect exercise of the will'. Samuel Solly recognized the affliction's physical roots in the nervous system and named the condition in 1860, warning doctors not to mistake it for a psychological malady. The steel nibs remained, and no one suggested doing any less scrivening.

A new technological revolution – mobile communications in all its forms – has radically changed life in less than two decades.

COVID-MADE EVERYTHING ONLINE

As with previous paradigm shifts, there are physical and mental elements, but now the machines are coming between us as social beings in entirely new ways. Algorithms designed to keep us engaged filter the world we see through our newsfeeds. Social circles have widened beyond our proximate community more than at any other point in history.

KW

Scrivener's palsy is now known as writer's cramp, and it is treated with botox injections in the hand. Retraining the muscles, including using different writing instruments, physical therapy or just swapping hands, has been shown to have a longer term therapeutic effect.

Samuel Solly (1805–71) was a British surgeon who urged his peers to examine the spinal cords of sufferers of writer's cramp post-mortem to find a cure for the cause. In 1865, he told an audience at St Thomas's Hospital that a disease of the spinal cord was 'the primary malady'. The search for a cure continues.

Algorithms are sets of rules or instructions, particularly those that are followed by a computer. In social media, they are used to find related content or to connect users with similar people in order to deepen their engagement with the network.

A Pen nib packets. Metal nibs boomed in popularity in the 1820s when manufacturers in Birmingham, UK, started mass-producing good quality, low priced, hard-wearing steel models.
B Ingenious inventors attempted to ease scrivener's palsy with pen-holding apparatus such as these from George Tiemann and Co. None addressed the core problem of repeated minute muscle strain.

While rates of mental health problems have been stable for adults in the past few years, emotional disorders among children and young people have increased more than 40% since 2004, to their highest point since records began.

YOUTH — new/young generation is leading the world.

The question of whether there is a direct causal link between technology and our minds' healthy functioning is an urgent one that needs to be addressed.

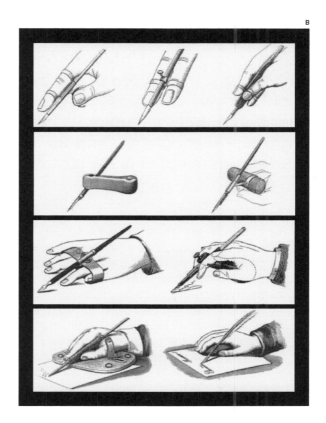

A

This book will primarily deal with modern technology. Our current wave of innovation tends to be highly personal, interactive and digital. It is designed to be habit-forming and integrated into every moment of the day. Rather than physically useful objects such as aeroplanes and street lights, our mobile devices and services focus on communication and interpersonal relationships with groups, trends, ideas and individuals. They might not give you phossy jaw or risk breaking your bones, but their ubiquity has introduced new fears over technology's impact on our health. Is this fear justified, or is the picture more complex?

Technological progress has always brought health and well-being coupled with disease and confusion, as engineers and designers work to address initial problems. Neolithic farmers experienced more physical problems than their Mesolithic forebears, but once the Copper Age arrived life expectancies had improved on the Stone Age, and doubled by the Iron Age. Choleric factory towns grew into safe, clean, comfortable housing once waste disposal, pest control and sanitation problems had been solved. Throughout the 19th century, rural farmworkers' diets were static, consisting mainly of bread with a little tea and sugar (even allowing for self-provisioning from gardens), while the new class of urban factory workers and miners saw living standards improve and diets broaden as their incomes rose. Malnutrition fell. Mass-produced, cheaper medical instruments could be used in the service of a greater number of people.

Mental health has benefited from advancements, too.

We cannot see rates of depression or anxiety from archaeology, as we can rickets or tooth decay, but we can see what is happening now. It is undoubtedly the case that many people are suffering from the effects of what US writers Alvin Toffler and his wife Heidi call 'future shock' in their 1970 book of the same name – anxiety produced by too much changing too fast – but it is also true that links between people at great distances have never been easier to maintain, and new communities are being found with little or no need to take geography into account.

Phossy jaw refers to the brain damage and jaw disfigurement found in people who worked with white phosphorus, mostly match makers, between 1839 and 1906, when the use of phosphorus in match production was banned.

Alvin Toffler (1928–2016) collaborated with his wife, Heidi (1929–2019), to write a series of books on the future. Titles include *Future Shock* (1970), *The Third Wave* (1980) and *Powershift* (1990).

B

C

In the 20th century, for the first time, technology was developed that was deliberately designed to affect the way we think and perceive the world, and we now use it continually. When it works, it boosts our mental well-being, even our intelligence, but it has entirely new ways of harming us, too.

In 1945, a man called Vannevar Bush (1890–1974) had been head of the US Office of Scientific Research and Development for four years, throughout the US involvement in World War II. He was in charge of the scientific war effort and was one of the most broadly knowledgeable technologists of his time. He published an article titled 'As We May Think' in the *Atlantic* in July 1945 on a subject he had been thinking about for more than ten years. It was an aide for researchers, a kind of sophisticated desk he called the memex.

The memex user was to scan their notes and important documents into the desk, linking them together by attaching keywords rather than using a central index. As the researcher referred back to their records, they would be able to follow those keywords to recall more data, being led through their work on a trail of linked information in an imitation of the way memories trigger deeper memories in the human mind. In short, the desk became a shareable extension of the researcher's own memory. This concept of a web of linked data and documents

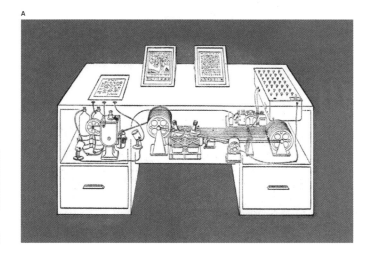

A

A Bush's memex drawing. Despite its influential status, no one built a working memex until 2014, when engineer Trevor F. Smith made one as a fun project with his daughter, Sparks Webb.

B Thad Starner and his wearable computer at MIT in 1997, and below with the Media Lab's Perceptual Computing Group. He is an engineer of wearable computers that augment human capabilities, such as Google Glass.

B

'As We May Think' sketched out a highly prescient collaborative vision for science, focused on understanding rather than destruction, and able to act as a healing process after the horrors of war. It was reprinted after the atomic bomb was dropped on Japan later that year.

Tim Berners-Lee (b. 1955) published his proposal for the World Wide Web in 1990 while working at CERN, the particle accelerator in Switzerland. He launched the first website, http://info.cern.ch, in 1991.

was to become the foundation of information sciences throughout the second half of the century, leading directly to the development of the World Wide Web by Tim Berners-Lee in 1990.

The web, together with many other applications that link computers and knowledge together, is intended to be an augmentation of human intelligence, what Apple CEO Steve Jobs (1955–2011) called a 'bicycle for the mind'. It is in our phones, our social networks, the websites we visit and the apps we use habitually all day, every day.

Computers and mobile phones have been a lifeline to isolated people everywhere.

A

From the lonely teen finding a peer group on Snapchat to the new parent scrolling through Facebook as they endure yet another night feed, they can be a great defence against loneliness and thereby reduce the stress of a cut-off situation.

The Internet has been the most common place for same-sex couples to meet since 2001, and the same is very likely to be the case for heterosexuals within years. Married couples who met online report a small but significantly higher level of happiness than their compatriots who met in the pub or at work and, while marital problems are associated with depression, anxiety and substance abuse, a happy pairing can expect to live appreciably longer and healthier lives.

But do the advantages outweigh the disadvantages? Is our increased dependence on mobile communications, content algorithms and social media doing us more harm than good?

One person finds affirmation in the form of a supportive audience for their *Doctor Strange* fan fiction; another finds it in the welcoming but destructive arms of the far right, drawn in by a subversive code of memes and in-jokes. One is boosted by a self-help group that addresses their particular psychopathology and background;

another finds themselves egged on by the compounding forces of thinspiration videos, self-harm tutorials and misanthropist isolation cults, fed to them by automated suggested content lists and anonymous trolls, intent on taking revenge on a world they have rejected by making it as unpleasant as possible.

In affluent countries, living standards and healthy life expectancies are at all-time highs. Suicide rates have been low and stable for decades, averaging just over 10 deaths per 100,000 since the year 2000, compared to more than 20 in the second half of the 19th century. As technology crowds further and further into our personal lives, some of us find it impossible to thrive. Technology is harming us in certain specific ways that are likely to intensify if we continue on our current trajectory.

The questions are: what are those ways, how serious is the harm and, most importantly, what can we do about it?

Thinspiration has been a banned tag on Instagram since 2012, as it promotes extreme thinness and unhealthy behaviours. However the content continues to find its way online, as users locate alternative tags before the network blocks them too.

A Star Wars fans, a well established online community, congregate in Portmagee, South-West Ireland. Islands off the coast featured in *The Last Jedi* and people travel to be with others who share their interest in the films.

B OKCupid is just one of more than 7,500 dating sites. Others include UniformDating, Mullet Passions and Gluten Free Singles. eHarmony alone is responsible for 4% of weddings in the USA.

1. Fear of Technology

A

Around the world, up to 13% of the population experiences symptoms of electrosensitivity. The rate of this is highest in Taiwan, and lowest, just 1.5%, in Sweden. Sufferers report a range of problems from headaches and nausea to heart palpitations and depression. They attribute this to the presence of radiation from Wi-Fi hotspots and mobile phones, both masts and handsets.

A   Electrosensitivity sufferers such as Jean-Jacque and Emilie sometimes resort to home-made shielding devices such as headscarves, sheets or, in this case, coats, lined with metal mesh or foil shields.

B   Many who experience the syndrome have to leave cities and live isolated rural lives away from people using technology and mobile devices that emit radio waves, and protect themselves when they have to visit towns.

In addition to these feelings of ill health, many people fear a link between mobile phones and cancer. Microwave radiation has been at the centre of cancer scares since the 1980s, when microwave ovens became more widespread in people's homes. Regulations to make sure the ovens could not continue to emit radiation when the door was open exacerbated fears, despite reassurances that the rules were intended to prevent people burning themselves. Studies that have found no link between microwave use and cancer, such as the comprehensive survey undertaken by Peter Valberg for *Cancer Causes and Control* in 1997, have not been enough to dispel the myth. Wi-Fi and mobile phones both use microwave spectrum radio waves, so the association is easy to carry over.

In Taiwan in 2013, a cohort study of 23 million people found no link between cancer and phones. In the same year, a Cancer Research UK-funded study of 791,710 women in Europe reached the same conclusion. Yet individuals continued to be electrosensitive. They genuinely felt ill unless wearing protective clothing, and they felt relief when they moved away from Wi-Fi and mobile phones.

Radio waves, light, Wi-Fi, mobile phone signals and kitchen microwaves are all the same kind of electromagnetic rays. They are different wavelengths and carry different amounts of energy however, meaning Wi-Fi and mobile phone signals cannot achieve the same warming effect as microwaves.

A **cohort study** takes a group of people who share a characteristic – in this case heavy mobile phone use – and measures certain things about them over time. Unlike a controlled trial there is no control group without the characteristic tested for comparison. They are particularly useful for refuting a cause and effect relationship.

B

Scientists tested whether the symptoms continued when the mobiles and routers were actually emitting something, or just appeared to be. There was no difference. Cancer rates were monitored for spikes in heavy phone users and IT workers: no difference. Mobiles have been ubiquitous for two decades and although brain tumour diagnosis rates have risen, researchers agree that this is down to better detection and reporting rather than an increase in incidence. The radiation given off by Wi-Fi routers and mobile phone masts and handsets is too low powered to harm our DNA and does not cause cancer or other ill health effects.

Routers generate Wi-Fi signals and thus connect wireless devices to the Internet.

Tabloid headlines persist, however, and support groups continue their well-meaning but misguided work, despite the NHS in Britain, the NIH in the USA and cancer research charities publishing guidelines that give evidence-led information. The World Health Organization classification of Wi-Fi in 2011 as a 'possible risk' did not help reassure anyone, but it was not intended to mean that any risk was actually present, only that there was some effect shown in tests on animals. Human exposure would never reach the power levels used in those experiments.

A

A Mobile phone masts have become a common feature of urban landscapes. The objections to them are sometimes aesthetic rather than health-based, leading to attempts to disguise them as local flora.

B Apple Store sales assistants in Russia happily welcome the latest models of iPhone. Queues still appear at shops all over the world every year when new technology becomes available.

B

To dismiss electrosensitivity because it is psychological in origin is over-simplistic and more than a little heartless. These people are genuinely suffering. What is really going on here?

It is not the case that all of these people would be feeling ill anyway and are blaming the technology for existing symptoms. They start to feel ill when the technology is introduced and feel better when it is gone. The fact that there is no physical link between their symptoms and their phone, for example, is beside the point. It is not just worry; they are sick and technology caused their ill health, but not in the physically causal way that would make such sickness universal. Why does technology adversely affect some people when others keenly queue up to get their latest dose of progress, and feel nothing but joy when they get it?

A

A No evidence on effects peculiar to the latest 5G mobile phone standard has yet been collected, but protesters already claim that new health problems are being felt.

B Marches such as this one in Germany in 2019 have coincided with cities such as Brussels, Belgium, and Geneva, Switzerland, delaying their rollouts of the antennas required for 5G reception.

Anxiety is the most common mental illness of all and can have a wide range of causes. Some are physical, some not. Researchers at Harvard in 2012 found that a third of the population will experience anxiety. Together with depression, dysregulated mood, aggression, fatigue and difficulty concentrating, there is a catalogue of mental well-being problems that are reported by sufferers as being in reaction to technology. What is it about the people who do not suffer from electrosensitivity that is inoculating them from it?

The electrosensitives, just like the civil servants who blamed the steel nibs for scrivener's palsy, are displaying a human trait that, when applied in other directions, has been a driver of progress. They are observing an effect and looking around for a pattern to explain it.

B

Diverging with the scientific application of pattern spotting, though, they are finding something new and, if it fits with concepts they already hold, they believe that it is the cause of the effect. Controlled trials that use logic and evidence to establish possible cause, such as the landmark British government-funded study published in the *Environmental Health Perspectives* journal in 2007 that found no link between ill health and mobile phone masts, are dismissed if they conflict with intuition. Science stands out as one of the very few areas of life where this evidence-led approach is taken. In politics, the arts, most of the humanities and our personal lives, this reliance on intuition is absolutely the norm.

Too often we forget that all technology, from the invention of fire onwards, was once new technology and that cutting-edge inventions have often provoked a fearful reaction. Poet John Keats (1795–1821) fretted that public money would be wasted on the 'nothing of the day' – the velo-cipede. 'We shall soon be nothing but transparent heaps of jelly to each other,' said the *New York Times* about the telephone in 1877.

Anxiety, in a clinical sense, includes panic attacks, debilitating phobias and a sense of the overwhelming need to escape. The pulse rises, muscles tense and the anxious person becomes vigilant, as if in anticipation of danger.

Dysregulated mood refers to mood swings that the subject cannot control, including anger and outbursts of temper. When dysregulation persists for most of the day, every day, for at least 12 months it can be classified as a clinical disorder.

Intuition is the tendency to seek out information that accords with our existing beliefs. To disregard everything else is called confirmation bias.

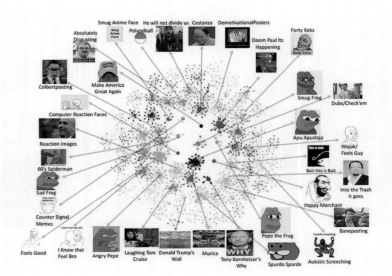

A

Sociologists of online behaviour have long since identified the brutalizing effects of assuming an anonymized persona on murky Internet forums full of trolls, such as 4chan and Reddit, and seen the dehumanization of people in opposing tribes there. For the average channer, normies are not a group of people with lives, families and feelings but transparent heaps of jelly, to be triggered and abused with glee and malice.

Influencers on social media can also have a huge impact on the views of followers without their realizing it. In the *Data & Society* report 'Alternative Influence: Broadcasting the Reactionary Right on YouTube', published October 2018, researcher Rebecca Lewis highlighted how audience members could be 'incrementally exposed to, and come to trust, ever more extremist political positions'. The data revealed the wide network of influencers collaborating with one another and acting as conduits to other influencers in the network.

A   A diagram showing how memes spread on fringe websites such as 4chan, Reddit and Gab. Some are racist, such as Happy Merchant, some triumphalist, such as Dubs, and some mock emotions.

B   This grinning face is used online to assert that another user is trolling – posting purely in order to create conflict. The crossed out version symbolizes the phrase 'Don't Feed the Trolls', i.e. resisting rising to the trolls' bait. However there is some doubt as to whether this tactic works, or whether online harassers will continue, or even escalate, their behaviour when they do not get the attention they seek.

4chan is a message board website where anonymous users gather to discuss subjects including Japanese animation, video games, far right politics and anti-feminism. Freedom of speech absolutism is taken as a given and contributors compete to find new ways to offend normal society. Similar platforms include 8chan and Gab.

Reddit is a website for posting links, discussing them and voting for your favourites. As with 4chan, unfettered speech is valued highly and trolls are common, but there are spaces for more mainstream and less offensive topics.

Normies, also referred to as 'normalfags' in 4chan's casually homophobic slang, are people who do not go to 4chan. Those who visit 4chan are known as 'anons', referring to the site's completely anonymized nature.

Neo-Luddites were attempting to reclaim the word 'luddite' which had come to mean crassly technophobic. The original English Luddites (active from 1811 to 1816) were concerned not with new technology per se, but its use in putting skilled weavers out of work.

In the 1990s, a group of people calling themselves the Neo-Luddites gathered around the writings of Chellis Glendinning (b. 1947), a psychotherapist specializing in recovery from trauma. She took the view that technology itself is not an evil, but that the current state of the technological landscape is harmful to many. She argued that all new technology should be critiqued and, if found wanting from the point of view of human well-being and ecological sustainability, abandoned and an alternative path found. All technology is political, she claimed, and creates social structures around itself that aid the preservation of the technology, rather than benefit the users.

B

A　Hillary Clinton is seen on multiple screens during her presidential candidate's debate with Donald Trump in 2016. Her campaign worked hard to make sure she was seen as often as possible.

B　Li Na was one of China's top tennis players until her retirement in 2019. The game's growth in China is largely due to her and her 23 million followers on Weibo, a website similar to Twitter. She is seen here on multiple screens in an airport, highlighting the prevalence of screens in everyday life.

C　Theodore Kazcynski being interviewed at the Federal ADX Supermax prison in Colorado, USA, in 1999. He is still imprisoned there, serving a life sentence without the possibility of parole.

Glendinning's *Notes Toward a Neo-Luddite Manifesto* (1990) conducts that critique and sets out a programme for the future without six particular types of technology – nuclear, chemical, genetic engineering, television, electromagnetic and computer – that are condemned as being negative, anti-people and likely to lead to the destruction of all life. Community-based renewable energy sources, organic technology inspired by nature, conflict resolution technology and decentralized social technologies are approved as being positive and life-enhancing.

For the Neo-Luddite, techno-logical progress should continue, but only in the approved directions and the rest of it should be stopped.

The ideas are not entirely new, continuing a tradition dating from the Arts and Crafts movement in Britain (1880–1920), and including the ideas of E. F. Schumacher (1911–77), especially those espoused in *Small Is Beautiful* (1973). Glendinning provides a lucid path to a peaceful future with well-being as its primary focus. However, to one particular individual she appeared to be foretelling an impending disaster to be fought against at all costs.

Unabomber derives from the acronym UNABOM (University and Airline Bomber), which was used by the FBI to refer to the lone wolf bombing case before they deduced Kaczynski's identity.

'Industrial Society and its Future' was published in full in the *New York Times* and the *Washington Post* in 1995 after Kaczynski said he would desist from terrorism if they did so.

Theodore Kaczynski (b. 1942) is better known as the Unabomber. He sent 16 bombs through the post in the USA between May 1978 and April 1995. Three of his targets were killed: Hugh Scrutton, a computer shop owner in Sacramento, in 1985; Thomas Mosser, an advertising executive in New Jersey, in 1994; and Gilbert Brent Murray, a lobbyist, also in Sacramento, in 1995. Most of his victims were scientists, technologists, airline staff or engineers. Kaczynski was trying to destabilize modern society to bring about a new set of technological norms in a twisted, murderous reflection of the Neo-Luddite project. He wrote a manifesto, 'Industrial Society and its Future', in which he set out his contention that technology has been disastrous for the human race, and that we are addicted to its comforts.

c

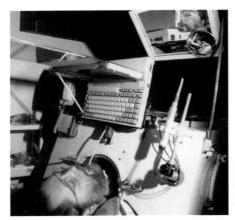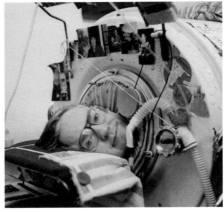

A

Transhumanism is a term coined by Julian Huxley in a lecture in 1951, drawing on a paper by W. D. Lighthall from 1940. It refers to the desire to evolve away from the current human condition via the use of technology.

Superintelligence will have been achieved when learning machines are more intelligent than people, a moment known among transhumanists as 'the singularity'. The eagerness with which it is looked forward to was satirized by writers Charles Stross and Cory Doctorow, who called it 'the rapture of the nerds' in their 2012 novel of the same name.

Ray Kurzweil (b. 1948), a pioneering optimistic inventor, futurist and director of engineering at Google, quoted Kaczynski at length in his book *The Age of Spiritual Machines* (1999), in a passage subtitled 'The new Luddite challenge'. Kurzweil relates Kaczynski's prediction of a society in which artificial intelligence is increasingly used to make decisions for the welfare of individuals. The machines are controlled by a tiny elite and their decisions are accepted because they genuinely seem to offer a better outcome for living standards. Humanity drifts into a situation in which it finds it cannot turn off the machines, as doing so would be tantamount to suicide. In this society, physical needs are satisfied, children are raised in 'psychologically hygienic' conditions and everyone is kept busy, but they are reduced to the status of domestic pets for the machines.

Kurzweil is a transhumanist. He believes that technological progress will soon result in a techno-utopia in which we defeat our own mortality with the help of the learning machines we have invented.

Once artificial intelligence equals or surpasses that of the human mind, it will be able to design new machine minds, ever more intelligent than itself, resulting in increasingly rapid evolution towards superintelligence. The application of this machine superintelligence to human problems will result in them being solved far more easily than before and a new, much better, society will be born.

Kurzweil does not see Kaczynski's fear of reduction to pet status as an unavoidable fate, but takes his ideas seriously enough to discuss them. The road we are on, says Kurzweil, far from leading to cosseted slavery, is a road paved with gold and we are already past the point at which we could turn off the machines. For Kaczynski, the machines keep us from being free. For Kurzweil, our free choice to make and live with the machines, like our choice to live in society, augments us and makes us, and our world, better.

A   Robert McNamara and Mark O'Brien were both iron lung users. McNamara for muscular distrophy, O'Brien for the after-effects of polio. The iron lung was an early example of total life support extended over a longer period.
B   James Nall, paralyzed and told he would never walk again after breaking his neck, took 819 steps using this robotic exoskeleton in 2013.

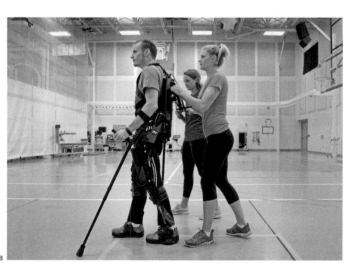

B

It is no wonder people feel anxious.

But the cause of the anxiety is unacknowledged by those who do not know how technology is progressing. Unless they understand what the machines are actually doing to them and their society, they can only blame partially grasped developments for their own feelings. That can never result in the kind of reasoned analysis that Glendinning believes is the way to build a healthier society. It can only lead to fear and uncertainty.

A Red dots clamour for the phone user's attention, regardless of how urgent the message is.

B A graph showing the adoption of different technologies in American households since the beginning of the 20th century.

A

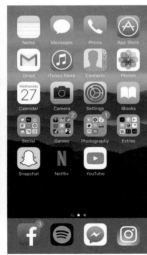
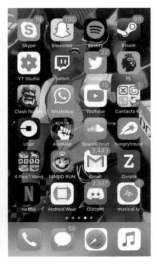

TECHNOLOGY ADOPTION IN US HOUSEHOLDS: 1903 – 2016

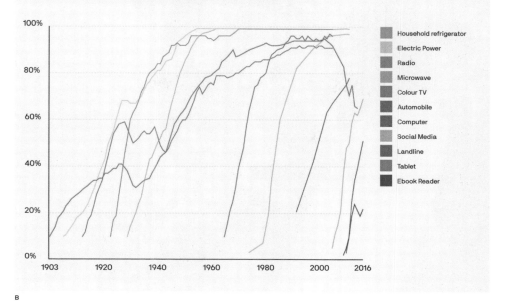

Household refrigerator
Electric Power
Radio
Microwave
Colour TV
Automobile
Computer
Social Media
Landline
Tablet
Ebook Reader

B

Almost all technological progress has happened in the last lifetime or two, especially since the invention of the computer, and the time between someone having an idea and that idea being disseminated around the world has shrunk so much that we have future shock. Alvin Toffler mapped out human history in terms of 800 lifetimes. Invention up until the last one or two spans of 80 years or so took place slowly over centuries. The developments of the wheel, fire, pottery, language, agriculture, the cart, even steam engines did not appear over a few years but took lifetimes to become widely adopted.

Things started to accelerate when the scientific method was developed by French philosopher René Descartes (1596–1650) in the 17th century. Building on the ideas of the 10th-century Iraqi-Egyptian astronomer and mathematician Ibn Al-Haytham (965–1040) and the 16th-century British philosopher Francis Bacon (1561–1626), Descartes rejected the platonic model of conducting science through a priori reasoning and insisted on using ruthless observation and experiment to discover the practical, actionable truth about the universe.

A

Then, in the 20th century, came mass production and the computer, with its amazing ability to analyse and communicate data. Millions of scientific papers were published, read and acted upon every year, and thousands of patents were granted. Major inventions arrived with unprecedented frequency and spread across the world at a previously unimaginable rate. Aeroplanes, space travel, computers, chemotherapy, robots, reliable contraception, nuclear power, antibiotics, recorded music, organ transplants and the Internet were all invented in the last two lifetimes, and are but a tiny fraction of the world-changing inventions of that period.

We are, undoubtedly, living in a time of change such as the world has never seen before. Our brains have evolved slowly over 2,000 years but we are having to negotiate a world that has changed inordinately over the last 200 years. Is it any surprise that we have new and confusing feelings about it all?

A Commuters use smartphones in Seoul, South Korea. 68% of South Korean adults have a smartphone.

B A Walkera test flight crew try out new virtual reality camera-equipped drones, allowing them to see where they fly and integrate virtual elements, such as games, routes and targets.

B

The pace of life accelerates for us every day, and if a person cannot cope with that acceleration they will feel that there is something terribly wrong with the world and their lives. If they do not understand where that feeling comes from, they can only ascribe it to sickness. Modern technology, as we will see later, actively works to conceal its existence from its users, and so they have little hope of understanding its workings. If we are to change the way we cope with change itself, and we must if we are to be at ease with progress, then the change need not be in the nature of technology, only in its transparency to those who adopt it.

A

Agriculture very clearly improved the lot of the overwintering Stone Age human, no longer hungry in the long months before spring, but the benefits were less clear to those who died of leprosy caught from their newly domesticated animals.

Neo-Luddites would say that the benefits of computerized communication are similarly unclear when the stress of always being available to work, unwanted social pressures and the pull away from time spent with the family are added into the equation.

Whether or not they are correct can only be determined by thoroughly understanding technology and what it does to us, which means taking an evidence-led approach.

There are many people who agree, more or less, with the Neo-Luddites, on a spectrum of acceptance and awareness. At the minimal end are the majority of people who prefer paper books or newspapers to e-books and websites, and paper voting cards to electronic machines, moving up along a sliding scale, shedding people as it goes: people who prefer business meetings to Skype calls; people who attend live music more than they listen to recordings; people who buy CDs rather than stream music; people who do not own a car; people who do not own a smartphone; people who do not have a landline; people who hand-write letters rather than send emails; people who cut off their electricity and draw their water from a well.

A   FOMO – 'Fear Of Missing Out' – is such a widespread feeling that this Australian music festival makes a virtue of only having one stage, so there's no chance of something good happening while you're elsewhere.

B   This community at Tinkers Bubble in Somerset, UK, uses scythes to cut crops, fells trees by hand and cuts timber using horse-drawn sawmills. They grow organically certified crops using no-dig methods and sell their produce, including butter, jam, honey, wine and cheese, at local markets. Photographed here by Ed Gold, they describe themselves as 'money poor but otherwise rich'.

B

A

The need to control technology is common to all of these people, but only those who understand it will be able to feel the all-important self-determination, crucial for any sense of well-being. In self-determination theory, human psychological needs are dependent on three factors: relatedness (connection with other people), autonomy and competence. Surrendering to our fears about new technology robs us of our autonomy and reduces our sense of competence. Self-determination is not a frivolous desire that we should suspend in order to allow technology to improve our lives, even when it seems clear that it would do so given our immediate problems.

We will always try to find a reason for our sickness, because we are problem-solving animals who will attempt to find a way out of any trap we are in. Sometimes that reason will be clear, and sometimes it will be necessary to deduce it from slim evidence. When the evidence is not sufficient, we will often still blame something, despite not really being able to be certain.

Self-determination theory grew out of work by Edward Deci and Richard Ryan in the 1970s and 80s. They identified three basic psychological needs that must be satisfied to allow optimal function and growth: competence, relatedness and autonomy. If these needs are met, our natural tendency towards self-motivation and integrated functioning can thrive.

New technology is unlikely to explain itself. When it arrives as quickly as it is at present, there is no time to make everyone understand.

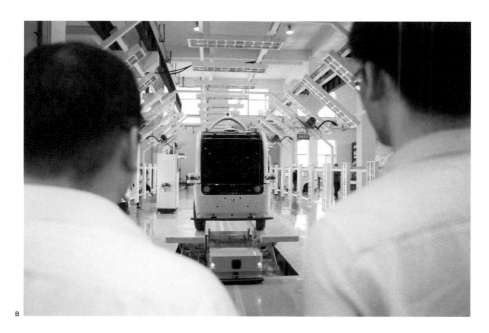

When an analytical algorithm is the technology in question, commercial imperatives require that no one outside the company can precisely understand it. Without transparency, backed by law and public testing, we have no reason to trust the motives of the big tech companies. We use their apps and websites because they are useful and compelling but we feel uncomfortable in a way that we do not with regulated technologies such as cars or medicines. Our social lives exist in a place in which we cannot relax.

Without understanding, the user cannot exert proper control over their use of a technology, or experience self-determination. We rush forwards into the future, ill prepared and ill informed.

A

A Edward Snowden speaks to a round table on the protection of whistleblowers at the Council of Europe in Strasbourg, France, in 2019. Snowden revealed large-scale surveillance by the American government in 2013.

B An attendee at the Google I/O developer conference contemplates the connections between musical artists as meticulously catalogued, dissected and presented in one of the apps on display.

C Amazon and LG executives unveil the Instaview ThinQ fridge, which has a large screen to re-order goods from Amazon and can suggest recipes based on what it knows it has inside itself.

With no clear authority that we trust and no information to guide us, we fall back on what we have been told without properly questioning it, take comfort from repeating what has become a superstition and come to rely on falsehoods. This has no therapeutic value in itself, but stepping outside it generates anxiety. In the absence of rare physical causes of harm it is this cycle of ignorance, attribution and superstition that upsets our mental well-being, and makes us sick.

2. Living with Technology

A

Technology pervades every area of our lives: our work, day-to-day living and leisure.

The working environment has always been a driver of both technology and tech-related sickness. We might avoid the brown lung syndrome of mill workers now that most of our jobs take place in offices, but there are other problems to contend with. Our aching backs and strained eyes might be immediate causes of worry but our furrowed brows, enfeebled muscles and cholesterol levels should probably concern us more.

Physically demanding workplaces in Europe, the USA and much of Asia are now heavily regulated. Lifting limits, training, protective equipment and risk assessments all do a good job of minimizing risk. The number of people receiving fatal injuries as a result of their work has reduced by 85% in the last 40 years alone, and work-related ill health in general has more than halved.

Mental health, however, enjoys few legal protections. There is no impetus from the state or mandatory risk assessment for insurance cover when estimating the mental health implications of changes in technology. Investigating the effects of technology on mental health has therefore been very much an academic rather than industrial pursuit. Trade unions and human resources professional bodies, such as the Chartered Institute of Personnel and Development in the UK, have all produced guides to beating work stress and sponsor academic research.

Unfortunately, as the ways in which devices are used at home and at work are so similar – the only difference is what is on the screen – lawmakers have shied away from looking too closely at the health effects of modern technology.

A   Filmgoers at a 4DX cinema in Moscow, Russia. As well as 3D glasses, the seats shake, wind blows and rain splashes over the audience. 3D and 4DX advancements boosted Russian box office revenue by 1,200% in four years.

B   Social media celebrities are the superstars of our day. Kylie Jenner is the world's youngest billionaire from selling makeup to her c. 150 million Instagram followers.

At work, at school and at home, owning a smartphone means that you are always in contact with your peers. This can be a wonderful thing, effective against loneliness and social isolation, as well as increasing productivity when managed properly. However, it is also a root cause of stress: being always on, never done.

A   Huawei research and development workers take time away from the screens at their desks to get lunch at the staff canteen, whiling away the time in the queue on their phones.

B   Demonstrators in Hong Kong hold up their smartphone torches. Mobile phones, along with social media, have become indispensible tools to self-organizing groups of protesters all around the world.

Christina Nippert-Eng divided the world into two in her 1996 paper 'Calendars and Keys: The Classi-fication of "Home" and "Work"'. There are segmenters and there are integrators. Segmentors cut themselves off from work as they leave the office, integrators take it home. A Google study in 2016 found the same distinction for

A

smartphone users. Segmentors turn their phones off on their way home from work and concentrate on home matters. Integrators carry theirs with them and attend to work with varying degrees of attentiveness. Some integrators very occasionally have a look, others stay glued to their screens, grunting at their children if they have done something particularly praiseworthy.

Segmentors have a simpler time. They note no difference between having a smartphone and not, because for them there is no difference. Integrators report a higher degree of work-related stress at home but also a greater ability to balance the demands of work and family or social life. Clearly, integrators have a more difficult plan to execute, but their feelings of competence are enhanced when they get it right.

There are many consultants who recommend turning phones off on the way home, and who offer coaching in how to reduce demand on workers away from the office in order to get the most from them during working hours. That is, of course, a very good way of operating for many people, but it prevents others from using their best time for work.

Teenagers have been found to have body clocks that are up to three hours out of sync with adult waking hours. Expecting a 16-year-old to get to school for 9 a.m. can be the equivalent of a 6 a.m. start for their parents, and sending them home at 3 p.m. is like an adult's afternoon off after an early start. Night owls of all ages have to stretch their days well over normal working times just to take advantage of their wide-awake evenings, while not getting fired for perpetual lateness, and larks have to squeeze everything in as quickly as possible before they start to feel sleepy after lunch.

A These Huawei development engineers in China are resting during their lunch breaks, watching videos on their company phones or catching up on sleep without ever leaving the office.

B More than five million people work in call centres exactly like this one in the top three countries in the industry alone: the USA, India and the Phillipines.

Mobile work devices have the potential to make working hours better for everyone, but, while core working hours are still ruled by the clock, devices can invade sleep and make everything worse. Sleep is one of the best things anyone can do to care for their health, and there is evidence that technology can disrupt it. Less stress is reported when smartphones are deliberately excluded from use in the bedroom.

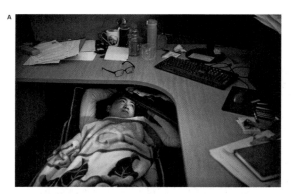

A

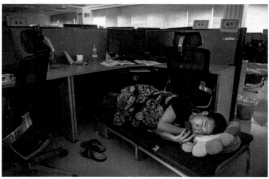

Body clocks, or circadian rhythms, are the natural cycle of the body that governs sleep, wakefulness and other daily biological routines. Some people are more awake earlier in the day, some later.

Night owls make up roughly 20% of the population, preferring to rise after 10 a.m. but happily burning the midnight oil. An equivalent percentage of people are 'larks', preferring an early start and an early night. Perhaps unsurprisingly for parents, surveys have found that children under the age of ten are more likely to be larks, but after puberty many turn into owls.

B

The feeling of being 'always on' is not unfounded, conjured into existence simply by the presence of the work-provided mobile phone. The modern work environment is dominated by one thing that drives employees' state of mind: monitoring.

Take, for example, the call centre: the epitome of the modern workplace. As the mill was to the 19th century, so a large, sparsely decorated, cheaply carpeted open office filled with people wearing headsets and talking as they type is to the 21st. The conditions of the call centre are replicated throughout other corporate structures, whether they are involved in data entry and customer care work or not. Software developers, medical teams, academics, lawyers and newsrooms have all learned from the call centre experience and cost control techniques.

A

B

Henry Ford (1863–1947) built a moving assembly line at his car plant in Michigan, USA, in 1913. While not the first example of mass production, Ford's dedication to efficiency made it a turning point in factory design.

Basecamp and **Jira** are both modern agile software planning tools. Project managers can communicate with their teams, set goals and assign tasks and developers can submit code for review and deployment, all through a single interface. Work thus becomes highly traceable and monitored by default.

The flat organizational structure, relatively small level of employee autonomy and close management of team members all contribute to what the sociologists Phil Taylor and Peter Bain called the 'assembly line in the head', the feeling of an inexorable stream of work flowing towards each member of the team, and the pressure to eliminate 'unproductive' time. Call centre teams are not 'teams' in the true sense of work being shared and coworkers communicating to complete a task, but pseudo teams in which tasks are broken up by managers or automated systems and routed to the available human resources in order to maximize productivity. Targets are shared to increase the feeling of responsibility on each individual to their colleagues.

In the call centre, the task is making individual calls. For a software developer, it might be a certain feature of an app, to be merged into the whole once it is ready for testing. For the medical worker, it might be providing the particular aspect of treatment their role demands for a single patient. Academics share authorship of their papers among hundreds of colleagues and newsrooms are as fragmented as any car plant.

This modular method of team working, closely monitored at every point through analysis of project objectives or through input of raw materials (information, calls, patients) into products (news, resolutions, health) for quarterly or annual assessment, does not leave any time for individual space or variation. This is not by accident. It is designed in this way so employees are more fungible and the variation of headcount to meet expected demand is more effective. US industrialist Henry Ford took the radical step of employing people to spot check worker efficiency using stopwatches. Now, it is very unusual to find a modern workplace of any size that does not constantly measure every worker, all the time. The 'assembly line in the head' is simply the internalization by the worker of the workplace design.

A   In Amazon's packing and distributon centre in Großebersdorf, Austria, the speed at which this employee works is entirely determined by the automated production line he works on.

B   In April 2019 Amazon workers in Berlin, Germany, tired of targets set by machines, took industrial action to demand better working conditions. 'We are humans not robots,' reads their banner.

C   Amazon has patented, but not yet implemented, a bracelet that would track the movements of their workers and buzz when they put their hands in the wrong place or took too long with an order.

The mental assembly line, unlike the physical one, does not necessarily stop when the worker leaves the building. As the triggers to action are largely delivered by software in the form of email alerts, internal instant messages or entries on project management tools such as Basecamp and Jira, they can be carried in the pocket to homes, bars, theatres and nursery pickups.

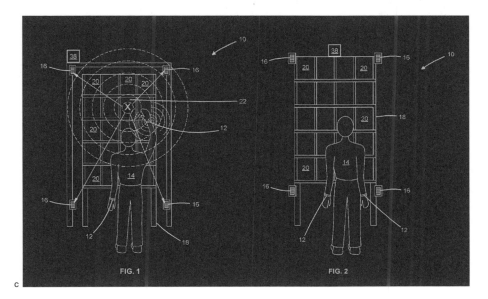

FIG. 1   FIG. 2

A   White Light Emitting
    Diodes (WLEDs),
    commonly used in
    LED displays such
    as phones and
    computer screens,
    actually have a
    distinct blue tinge,
    peaking significantly
    around the 450 nm
    wavelength. Screen
    manufacturers use
    yellow phosphor
    filters to correct
    this, with varying
    degrees of success.

In addition to the eye strain, vocal loss, musculoskeletal damage, hearing impairment and bowel problems experienced by call centre staff, the workplace illness common to all mental assembly line workers is stress. Individual working pace is, deliberately, subjugated to the pace of the team, and too great a mismatch will be felt as uneasiness, moving through levels of severity that end in sickness. Mental and physical tiredness are by far the most common causes of complaint. Some 57 and 62%, respectively, of call centre workers say they experience these problems 'very regularly'.

Monitoring workers all the time makes work their constant natural state. When our factory floors extend to our bedrooms, stress-related illness is almost impossible to avoid.

A

On top of the presence of work stress in bedrooms at night, blue light in particular gets a bad press. A study in Spain has linked it with higher rates of breast and colon cancer, an article in the *Lancet* found an association with increased symptoms of bipolar disorder, and 2016 saw the journal *Molecular Vision* publish a wide-ranging round-up of the available evidence, suggesting the possibility of long-term harm and disruption of natural sleep cycles. Health features on news websites accompanied all of these studies, to be read late at night on mobile phones by increasingly panicked insomniacs.

None of the studies showed a direct link between the light and the various specific health effects, and the intensity of light coming from computer and phone screens is not enough to cause macular degeneration, but it is clear that blue light at night has a negative effect on sleep. Sustained loss of sleep, or even sufficient but poor quality sleep, can have serious implications for health. It can mean immediate problems such as poor memory function and an inability to concentrate, and also longer term issues with heart disease, diabetes, stroke, Alzheimer's disease, blood pressure problems and obesity.

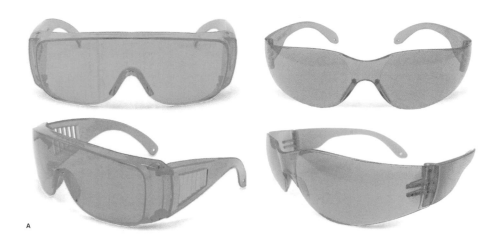

A

LED computer and phone screens, which tend towards the blue end of the spectrum, can inhibit deep sleep if used in the hours shortly before retiring. Dimming the screen or using a more yellow colour palette can make all the difference.

Researchers have found that LED screens reduce the release of melatonin, making it harder to sleep, but do not reduce feelings of tiredness. Interactive activity on electronic devices such as texting or social media messaging can increase stress levels late at night, thus making it more difficult to sleep, but passive activities such as watching a film or listening to audio do not. The nature of what is on the screen is what makes the difference, rather than the presence of the screen itself.

In this case, the compulsive nature of our technology is endangering our health. Checking our email, Twitter, Weibo, Facebook or any of the networks that draw us in unthinkingly one last time before bed robs us of our sleep, and sleep stops us from becoming ill. It fights off infection, orders what we have learnt that day and repairs our bodies. Any habit that stops us sleeping is disastrous for our health.

Sex, too, is suffering. Some 35% of Americans report having less sex at night if they take their phones, and therefore their work and social lives, to bed. Sex not only reduces stress at other times of the day, it guards against prostate cancer in men, loss of bladder control in women and boosts Immunoglobulin A (thought to aid the immune system) in everyone.

Outside our homes, the world we have built around our technology is not designed to make us fit.

A **yellow colour palette** is a feature of all recent smartphones and tablets. It is a special mode for late-night viewing (called night mode on Android and night shift on iOS), which moves away from the blue and gives the display a pleasantly sandy, sepia-toned filter.

Melatonin is produced by the pineal gland in the brain in the evening, starting at about 9 p.m. on average. As the level rises, people become drowsier and eventually fall asleep. This is separate from mental and physical tiredness from activity, and the two states can be out of sync, especially if melatonin levels are artificially depressed by the presence of bright light.

A   As companies capitalize on the health fears around blue light, it is possible to buy glasses that add an additional filter to your phone or computer's screen. Dimming or yellowing your screen would have the same effect.

B   Chinese teenagers attend residential camps designed to wean them off mobile phone and social media use that has become problematic.

C   This camp, in Huai'an, China, opened in 1997 but is now one of many all over the country. Independent figures on recovery rates are not available.

A

We live far from our places of work. As country dwellers moved to the city to work in factories, the cost of urban housing rose. City centres became prohibitively expensive, so people moved to the suburbs. Industrial estates grew up in old cities. Many new cities such as Brasília in Brazil and Chandigarh in India were planned with mandated zones for industrial and office activity far away from residential areas, making long commutes unavoidable.

We developed trains, trams, buses and cars to move us around every day in time for work, but few of us – 6%, down from 30% in 1900 – walk. Cycling miles are going up, but the number of trips is going down, which indicates a shift towards cycling being a hobby for people who want to get out for a long time.

In addition, the work we do is less active. Only 35% of UK jobs have a manual element, the rest comprised of sitting gazing at screens, talking to people on the phone, running meetings and lecturing. No one ever gained muscle by building a spreadsheet. Unpaid labour such as housework or caring for children or elderly relatives is also less physical thanks to household appliances, cars and public transport.

A   Hong Kong is the most expensive place in the world to buy a city centre apartment. In 2018 prices stood at more than £3,200 per square foot, double the price of a home in central London, UK.

B   Alibaba sales representatives work at their individual screens while larger screens display live updates of their team targets during a 'Singles Day' online sales promotion, similar to Amazon's Prime Day.

Shopping and chores such as banking are more likely to be taken care of online, meaning the stroll around the shops no longer burns off that little but regular bit of energy and our walking muscles go entirely unworked. This also cuts off a range of social interactions, from tiny hellos and nods to shopkeepers to accidental meetings with friends in the street, further isolating the already lonely and building up mental health problems in the vulnerable.

This chauffeured, desk- and house-bound population needs less fuel, but the amount of food available is going up and the cost per calorie is going down, leading to obesity.

Leisure choices have also increased our sedentariness. The number of people who class themselves as physically active has recovered a little in the past ten years, but it is still historically very low. Thanks to the availability of online entertainment, children are less likely to play outdoors, and their games are less likely to have a physical component. Activity tracking by Fitbits and smart watches, exercise reminder apps and outdoor computer games such as *Pokémon Go* or *Zombies, Run!* offer hope for a reversal of this trend but are, so far, minority pursuits.

Obesity is at an all-time high. 20% of people in Europe and 39% in the USA are obese. Obesity can lead to cancer, diabetes, stroke, heart disease and sleep problems, and can itself be a blocker to exercise.

A

Obesity is a medical condition. Medical professionals are moving away from body mass index (BMI) – the weight in kilograms divided by the square of the height in metres – as a definition of obesity, as it can falsely identify athletic people as overweight. For muscular people, waist measurement is used instead. Men with a waist of 94 cm (37 in.) or more and women with a waist of 80 cm (32 in.) or more might be in danger of suffering from weight-related illness.

Asian obesity rates are much lower, less than 2% in some countries, but Asian people tend to be more at risk from cardiovascular disease at lower BMIs because of their fat distribution patterns, and their activity levels are even lower than in the USA.

Someone who works, commutes, has non-sporting hobbies and takes very little exercise (that is to say, almost everyone, everywhere) is now heading down a road that leads to heart disease, vascular problems, type 2 diabetes, cancer and stroke.

Even before our technology reaches us, it has been the cause of sickness.

A   Two teams compete in the European League of Legends Championship (LCS) in 2017. In 2018 380 million people watched e-sports – competitive computer game playing – globally.
B   Chen San-yuan uses 29 mobile phones mounted on his bike and two handheld mobile phones to catch Pokémon in Taiwan.

B

A

Your mobile phone, for example, is very likely to contain tantalum, a mineral derived from an ore known as coltan. Coltan mining is an extremely dangerous and unhealthy business. The top countries for tantalum mining are Rwanda, the Democratic Republic of the Congo, Nigeria and Brazil, all of which have been found to overlook very poor health and safety standards from mining companies.

Coltan miners experience respiratory problems due to ore dust inhalation. The dust is radioactive, leading to an increased cancer risk. Instances of miners using their bare hands to dig have been found in the past, and protective breathing filters are not common.

Tantulum was discovered in 1802 by the Swedish chemist Anders Gustaf Ekeberg. Capacitors made from tantalum have a very high capacitance – they can store more charge – in a very small size, which is perfect for shrinking electronics. They are also resistant to corrosion and have a very low failure rate.

Coltan is just one of the many unhealthy minerals that slip into our devices unnoticed. The people such minerals make ill are a long way away in countries we imagine to be full of problems anyway, so reports of more are lost in the noise. Even when we are aware of health problems in manufacturing, we do not always want the products any less.

When we throw things away, we continue to ship our health issues abroad. In Britain, most plastic classified as recycling used to go to China, but a major campaign against *yang laji* – foreign rubbish – has now ended the acceptance of dirty plastics in Chinese ports. It had been piling up in landfill and acting as a vector for pests, skin diseases and forms of hepatitis, rather than being made into clean new materials.

A A *'creuseur'* (miner) in a cobalt mine in the Democratic Republic of Congo. Half of the world's cobalt comes from the DRC, to be used in electric car and laptop batteries.

B Much of the plastic delivered to Chinese ports before the *yang laji* ban was unsuitable or uneconomic to recycle, and workers had to hand sort it, sending much to landfill.

B

More than 35 million metric tonnes (38.5 million tons) of illegally exported and dumped electronics waste is arriving every year in countries including Nigeria, Pakistan, Ghana and Thailand, as well as China. Heavy metal poisoning has been recorded in people living near the dumps, and the new industry of 'informal mining' has grown up to raid these sites for valuable minerals, without any of the necessary safeguards to health.

Informal mining is the raiding of rubbish dumps and landfill sites for valuable materials such as old electronics or metals for recycling. Safety precautions against poisons and infections are very rare, and child labour is very common.

Tests near one of the big dump sites in Ghana, for example, found lead levels in the soil at 18,125 parts per million (the US EPA standard is 400 ppm) and blood and urine samples from people who foraged on the site were found to contain elevated levels of barium, cobalt, copper, iron and zinc. The dumps are part of a $52 billion electronics recycling industry. In 2015, political scientists George Bob-Milliar and Franklin Obeng-Odoom called the informal mining activity 'an employer, a nuisance and a goldmine'.

A

B

A A labourer works at Green Eco-Manufacture in Jingmen, central China. It is the country's biggest used home appliance recycling factory.

B A man hammers computer components while hand-processing electronic waste in West Bengal, India. Valuable minerals are recovered in this way but the processors risk exposure to toxic materials.

C Screens are a common occurrence during family time, even in countries with traditional family values such as Italy.

c

Our screen-dominated environments affect our minds as well as our bodies.

Every parent is aware of the effect that sitting in front of the television or playing computer games has on their children when they are very young.

At the time there is quiet, but afterwards there might be rage, lack of focus, aggression or unusual levels of clinginess. The parents and many psychologists agree: screen time must surely be near the top of the list of possibly harmful technologies. But look closer at the evidence and the phrase 'screen time' starts to be problematic. What is the child doing when they are looking at a screen? Are they playing a game? What kind of game? Are they reading a book on an e-reader or are they absorbed in a series of rapid-cutting cartoons and adverts? What exactly are we worried about here?

Settings   **Screen Time**

SCREEN TIME   Today at 11:50 AM
iPhone X
2h 7m

Social Networking   Creativity   Productivity
1h 19m   9m   7m

Downtime
Schedule time away from the screen.

App Limits
Set time limits for apps.

Always Allowed
Choose apps you want at all times.

Content & Privacy Restrictions
Block inappropriate content.

FAMILY

Today   Last 7 Days
iPhone X
SCREEN TIME   Today at 12:14 PM
2h 17m

Social Networking   Creativity   Productivity
1h 20m   9m   7m

MOST USED   SHOW CATEGORIES

Tweetbot ———— 46m

Messages —— 16m

Facebook — 13m

Settings — 12m

Photos — 9m

Today   Last 7 Days
iPhone X
SCREEN TIME   Today at 12:14 PM
2h 17m

Social Networking   Creativity   Productivity
1h 20m   9m   7m

MOST USED   SHOW APPS & WEBSITES

Social Networking ———— 1h 20m

Creativity — 9m

Productivity — 7m

Other — 6m

Reading & Reference — 1m

PICKUPS

6 per hour

Total Pickups   87
Most Pickups   26 between 11 AM – 12 PM

NOTIFICATIONS

143°   Around 11 per hour

Gmail — 61
Messages — 31
Ring — 22
Tweetbot — 8

A

In 2018 a huge survey called the ABCD study started. Researchers began tracking the brain development of almost 12,000 children, using MRI scans combined with interviews and social observation. The children's brain development will be monitored from the age of nine into early adulthood. Data from the work has already led reporters to infer that staying up late to play video games is a cause of poor attention and cortical thinning. The latter is a process that occurs naturally in everyone as they age; it is associated with depression, schizophrenia and Alzheimer's disease.

ABCD, though, is not designed to give definitive answers about causation, but to assist in building a model of average development. In fact, the purpose of the research is to gather a wide range of development studies that would allow scientists to filter out things that could be normal variation but appear to be associated with some particular activity. We will know more when it comes to an end in 2028.

There is evidence that media, especially films, are presented with shorter cuts between shots and presentations, but that does not mean that attention spans are getting shorter. Alerts and other inter-ruptions from computer programs, apps and our surroundings make it more difficult to focus on one activity, and in a world where we are likely to carry a few devices that can vie for our attention it will be more difficult to concentrate throughout the average day. However, the evidence says that once the devices are turned off we are just as able to stay on our mental targets as anyone from the pre-digital age.

A   Apple's Screen Time app has been included on all iOS devices since 2018, automatically tracking mobile phone use.

B   The Leapfrog My Own Leaptop is a children's version of the computers they see their parents using.

C   Ceanfly make a toy version of the device parents use even more than a laptop: a smartphone.

The American Academy of Paediatrics recommends no more than two hours of media, including video games, television, online videos and movies, per day. The figure has been repeated by the British NHS and the Royal College of Paediatrics and Child Health (RCPCH).

B

C

Importantly, none of these bodies found that it is the screens themselves that are the problem, but the way they displace activities such as talking to families, active play, study and, crucially, sleep. Few health bodies find a problem with e-reader time or video chat with distant relatives. The RCPCH called the displacement of other activities 'the main way in which screen time and negative outcomes may be linked'.

A survey of more than 120,000 adolescents analysed by Andrew Przybylski and Netta Weinsten in the journal *Psychological Science* in 2017 found that moderate use was not associated with mental problems, and there were even some advantages for well-being. The What About Youth survey in 2018, again of 120,000 adolescents, found that sleep and a good diet had far more of an effect on mental well-being than screen time, or even bullying.

When screen time prevents a child from playing outside with their friends, doing their homework or exercising, clearly there is a problem. But it is more useful to look at exactly what that person is doing, rather than the device they are doing it on.

A

A   Pupils testing products they have designed at the Robo School of Robotics, Kiev, Ukraine, where courses in robot engineering for ages six and up are run in evenings and school holidays.
B   Alex Boston is just one victim of online bullying. Alex's parents sued two of her classmates for setting up a false and malicious Facebook page claiming to be hers.

B

Snapchat and Instagram in the USA and Europe, and WeChat and Douyin in China, have become the media in which millions of young people conduct their social lives and build their identities. However, conducting a social life in the same space occupied by celebrities can lead to status anxiety. For example, the Instagram feed of Kylie Jenner, who entertains her millions of followers with highly polished and styled professional photographs, is bound to make one more aware of the shortcomings of one's own Instagram feed. The comparison is more direct than that which could be made between pre-digital teenagers and their pop star or actor idols, and so the feelings of inadequacy can be more acute.

A very clear case of an activity made worse by technology is one that has always been with children in some form: bullying.

A study of children reporting to hospitals with mental health complaints found that those who had been bullied online were more than eleven times more likely than those who had not been bullied at all to experience suicidal ideation. Those who experienced bullying in the flesh were eight times more likely. Suicide rates among teenagers, particularly in the USA, stable since the mid-1990s, began to increase in 2010 and have continued to rise ever since. A trend among many appears to be making itself clear.

Ideation is the formation of ideas and concepts. The ideas can range from considering a possibility to fully intentional planning.

Online bullying can be made more difficult to deal with as the online spaces can be hard for parents and teachers to access. This is part of their appeal for young people, who are happy to have conversations their carers cannot read in games and messaging apps. Research from the Oxford Internet Institute suggests that offline bullying is still more common, and that the core activity of targeting individuals for cruelty has the same roots whether it's in *Grand Theft Auto* online voice chat, Instagram comments, abusive targeted online polls or a corner of the playground, and that the solutions are also the same. In the case of technology, the most effective solution is for the adult responsible for the bullying child to cut off their access.

A

A   The 'I Am A Witness' campaign urges the large number of teenagers who witness online bullying to speak out. Its messages on mutual support and worth are the same as offline bullying interventions.
B   Sensevideo, a pedestrian and vehicle recognition system invaluable to surveillance, has made its maker SenseTime one of the world's most valuable startups.

B

Technology learns about its users from data collection, but only collects data on groups researchers choose to take notice of. Just 11% of executives in California's Silicon Valley are female, and this under-representation feeds into the technology produced.

As feminist writer Caroline Criado Perez (b. 1984) details in *Invisible Women: Exposing Data Bias in a World Designed for Men* (2019), the exclusion of women from data collection means that in a vast range of products they are not properly accounted for. For example, women are more likely to take a number of short hops on bus and train journeys to fulfil caring and household duties rather than simple A to B to A commuting journeys, and those broken journeys are tracked less well by machine-learning algorithms for route planning.

Bosses are less likely to notice the data gaps that do not personally affect them.

Minorities can be similarly overlooked; it took Jackie Alciné, a black software consultant, to point out on Twitter in 2015 that Google's Photos software identified black people as gorillas. This algorithm was never fixed, only blocked from labelling anything as a gorilla. According to Google's 2018 diversity report, only 2% of their US employees are black.

A

Technology has entered every part of our lives, from early years, through school, into adulthood at work and in leisure. No previous generation has been as fully immersed in a technological environment, or been so inured to digital monitoring that they become their own taskmasters. Neither has any previous generation benefitted from easy communication with such a large number of people who align with our interests and personalities.

We know what a lot of technology is not doing.

B

It is not giving us cancer from its light; it is not driving us mad simply by existing; it is not the reason we choose not to take any exercise or eat too much cake. It is, however, the means by which we feel ourselves to be constantly at work, and have ever more compelling forms of entertainment available to use in cheaper and more time-consuming ways, taking us away from intimacy with those who are close to us, sex and the health-giving benefits of physical play.

A   Customers waiting to go in to see a film on the big screen use their small screens in a multiplex cinema in Bangkok, Thailand.

B   Japanese commuters use their phones to read the news, stay in touch with people at home and do some of the work that they did not complete when they were still at their desks.

We know that some of our raw materials come from unsafe and unethical sources. We know that many of us are excluded from our technology working as well as it could because we are poor, uneducated or a woman. We also know that lack of sleep, internalized work practices and failing to allow for individual pace and rhythms can lead to stress, depression and anxiety. Dirty manufacturing, data gaps and sedentary lifestyles can lead to physical diseases.

All these problems are caused by aspects of our technology, and yet we continue to use it. Why do we do that?

3. Becoming Hooked

A

According to their market value, all of the top five public companies in the world in 2018 – Facebook (which includes Instagram and WhatsApp), Amazon, Alphabet (Google's parent company), Microsoft and Apple – made technology whose success depended on its habit-forming nature.

There are trillions of dollars at stake in finding the right thing that will make users pull out their phones and access a service while barely thinking about it. When something is that valuable, it is not going to be left to chance.

After graduating from Stanford University, US writer Nir Eyal (b. 1980) went to work in Silicon Valley, where he saw people building products that became habits. He observed, learnt from the successes, collected his findings and taught a course (back at his old university) on the science of influencing behaviour. The course became a book titled *Hooked: How to Build Habit-forming Products* (2013). It is now the bible for technologists hoping to win big by getting hold of their users' time without them being aware of it.

Hooked describes a cycle that takes the user from barely perceptible triggers that lead to tiny actions, up a spiral of commitment until they are happily spending hours on an activity to which they are giving very little thought. If you think this is not you, have a look at the amount of time you are spending on the apps on your phone. iOS calculates this data automatically, and there are plenty of Android apps that will work it out for you. Compare the amount of time you devote to your favourite app with the amount of time you would like to spend on that ambition or intention you have been carrying around but feel too busy for.

The Hook Model has four phases: trigger, action, variable reward and investment. We will take them one by one.

A A billboard advertises the debut of Facebook on the Nasdaq stock exchange in 2012. The company's value at flotation was reckoned to be $104 billion. In 2019 it was more than $500 billion.

B Netflix, the video streaming service, automatically plays the next episode in a series, so will run and run unless you stop it. To avoid playing out an entire box set if you fall asleep it will occasionally ask if you are still waching.

C A visualization of the metadata – information about information – that Netflix holds on 5,000 of the films in its catalogue, used in a $1 million competition to improve the suggested content algorithm called the Netflix Prize.

B

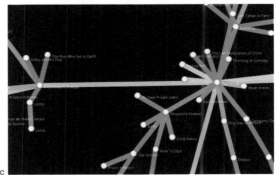

C

Triggers can be internal or external. They are anything that leads the user into the product. An external trigger could be an alert, a red dot on a phone screen icon, an email or a billboard. An internal trigger might be waking up in the morning, finding oneself performing a particular action such as feeding the cat or leaving the house, a pang of boredom or the passing of empty, nervous time.

Any of those triggers can lead to action. The user reads the email and follows a link. They click on the icon when they see the red dot. They relax after tackling something difficult and do something else to take their mind off it. In the past, this activity might have been making a cup of tea or watering the plants. Now, there are thousands of companies hoping it will be opening their app.

A Snapchat tracks 'streaks' – consecutive days on which users have sent each other messsages – and encourages engagement by rewarding longer streaks with badges.

B A simple diagram showing the triggers that form habits. Human psychology has always reacted to triggers with action, either mental or physical. Marketing has always exploited triggers, but they have rarely been so minutely analysed as they currently are.

A

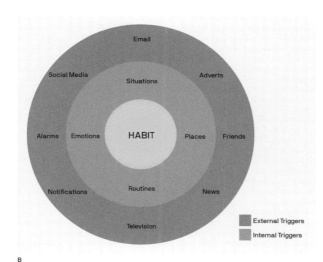

Billboard advertising is growing faster than any advert form apart from the Internet, and was a 38 billion dollar industry in 2018. Mobile phones give billboard advertisers a great deal of location data about their customers that they did not have in the past.

For a habit to start to form, the action has to be rewarded. If this is simply what the user expects then the action is unlikely to stick, but if the reward is surprising, while still being satisfying, then the user is more likely to come back. The fridge light coming on when the door is opened does not captivate us, but if there is a new and different treat in the fridge every time we go there, then we will return for more. Social networks have this variability built in by the actions of our friends: *Susie has posted a photo*, says the trigger. *Click*, goes the action. *Oh, Susie, look at what you have got yourself into now*.

To cement the habit, the user is required to do something – to make an investment. We click 'Like' on Susie's photo, or leave a comment, or post a picture of our own. We follow someone new, or block someone, or retweet something. We reply to an email, or create a wishlist, or add something to a shopping basket. We make a commitment.

A

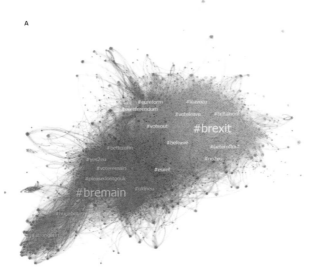

A   Mapping the occurrence
     on Instagram of various
     hashtags surrounding
     the Brexit debate in 2016.
     There was little overlap of
     the most extreme terms,
     suggesting that few users
     saw posts from people
     they disagreed with.
B   The elements of the
     Facebook and Instagram
     newsfeed ordering
     algorithms. The exact
     weighting of each of these
     factors in presenting
     content to users is
     a closely guarded
     company secret.

After that, we are triggered again – possibly externally in a more tailored way thanks to the information we handed over at the action and investment stages, possibly internally by our own growing inclination – and each time we go around the habit becomes more deeply ingrained, and the company that makes the app becomes a little more valuable.

The nature of the reward and the opportunity to make an investment are vital to the form that the habit takes and the consequences for our health. Each of the big companies monitor their users' activities and feed them more of what their algorithms calculate they are most likely to act on. Facebook, Instagram, Google News, Amazon, PornHub, YouTube, they all automatically conspire to create a bubble that reinforces a user's instinctive prejudices, predilections and fears.

A **bubble**, online, is the boundary marker of the content seen by a user. Website algorithms use the choices users make in order to feed similar content back to them and enclose them in an airtight but transparent seal.

Weaponization is the adoption of previously harmless or positive entities and their use to serve the ends of a particular group or company.

Search engine and social media optimization is the creation and modification of content to appeal specifically to search algorithms and users of big social networks in order to attract traffic. Spending on search engine optimization consultancy and development was estimated to be $72 billion per year in 2018 worldwide.

This reinforces political division between people in separate bubbles. It stops community being a supportive thing that helps us examine our choices and turns it into a compounding force, possibly with severe mental health consequences. Studies have found increased incidences of depression, anxiety, social isolation, eating disorders, compulsive disorders, gambling dependency and suicide all linked to habit-forming products. 'Social media is dangerous' is a misleading, simplistic headline, but the weaponization of community to drive engagement regardless of the health of the user is a real problem.

Groups that wish to influence our opinions or create content that attracts our attention have a great deal of interest in exploiting these algorithms, so they can get their pages and videos to the top of the lists. Entire industries – search engine and social media optimization – have grown up out of reading the runes and reverse-engineering the patterns that will promote their client's content over other people's. While they will give clues, Google, Facebook and the rest are absolutely locked up tight when it comes to explaining the precise levers that are being used to deliver their results.

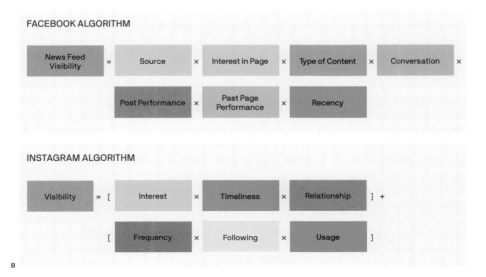

FACEBOOK ALGORITHM

| News Feed Visibility | = | Source | × | Interest in Page | × | Type of Content | × | Conversation | × |

| | | Post Performance | × | Past Page Performance | × | Recency | |

INSTAGRAM ALGORITHM

| Visibility | = [| Interest | × | Timeliness | × | Relationship |] + |

| | [| Frequency | × | Following | × | Usage |] |

Where normal community provides challenges for the individual, checking their assumptions, introducing contradictory evidence to their hypotheses and generally taking the mickey, this process of giving the user more of what they have already declared or shown that they like tends to feed their prejudices back to them. They are introduced to more people who feel the same way, shown content that backs up what they already think, and taken further. They seek out more content that they agree with. When they find themselves in a mutually confirmatory community, they see less reason to leave and their minds are less likely to be changed.

This looping mechanism goes beyond making the individual feel part of a larger whole and increases feelings of isolation. The further a lonely person turns to their online support network for relief, the stronger the feelings of distance from their proximate geographical community become, compounding their need for digital comfort. People have always gravitated towards groups in which they feel known, seen and supported, be that the Women's Institute, the local Conservative Club or the Black Panther Party. The difference is that online groups can be accessed at any time, providing a constant way out of challenging situations.

The draw is particularly strong if an individual's geographical community has become a focus of resentment. Incels, for example, are members of a largely online community of mostly young men, who believe that the world is weighted in favour of monogamous heterosexual romantic pairings, and that women's freedom to choose their own partners unfairly prioritizes the fulfilment of sexually attractive males. They consider themselves to be unattractive but still believe in male supremacy, and so resent the women they encounter for not giving them the sexual relief to which they feel they are entitled.

Incel is short for 'involuntary celibate'. Four mass murderers in the USA have been self-described incels. The first, Elliot Rodger, killed six people and injured fourteen more in May 2014 in Isla Vista, California, before committing suicide. On incel message boards, Rodgers is referred to as 'the supreme gentleman'.

A Santa Barbara County Sherriff Bill Brown with a press conference board showing a photograph of incel mass murderer Elliot Rodger and some of his weapons.

B Messageboard site 4chan allows users to post uncensored content anonymously, allowing it to become a haven for alt-right, racist and misogynistic users.

C When in 2014 some 4chan users felt the site was becoming too heavily moderated 8chan emerged as an alternative platform. However it was forced offline in 2019 following three mass shooters posting their manifestos on the site.

A   InfoWars is a conspiracy theory and right-wing comment website funded by sales of vitamins and survivalist equipment. It has been criticized for fuelling white supremicist sentiments within its large online following.

B   Clashes at the Unite The Right rally in Charlottesville, Virginia, where James Fields killed Heather Heyer when he drove into a crowd of counterprotestors.

C   Facebook employs tens of thousands of moderators worldwide, reviewing and blocking text and videos that have been reported for breaking the network's rules on violence and hate speech, but with 1.5 billion users they struggle to keep up.

Offered a choice between women they believe conspire against them with the men they envy and a group of online men who repeatedly tell them they are noble creatures being victimized by society, newly radicalized incels step further and further away from offline friendships into a destructive group that can be very difficult to escape.

Social media is far from being the only offender in this pattern.

Google searches also feed more of the same to searchers, tailoring results to bolster what has been clicked on by the user and people like them – that is to say, people who have clicked on those things, too. YouTube autoplays related videos with similar messages to the ones you have just watched, reinforcing what you have already seen and making it appear that there is a chorus of voices agreeing with even the most extreme views.

Even PornHub, the pornographic video aggregator, operates in the same way, reassuring its users that whatever flavour of sexual content they have searched for there must be plenty of others with similar taste. You are never alone when you have billions of individuals to build a group with.

The trend in online news consumption is moving away from individual sources into personalized streams of articles on social media, curated by our peers. Most people under the age of 25 list social media as their main source of news. It is not until we look at the over 45s that we start to see individual news companies favoured.

YouTube is a video sharing website, and has been a Google company since 2006. There is some evidence that YouTube's content promotion algorithm favours extreme content, as its learning algorithm has noticed the human tendency to watch more shocking titles whether we agree with them or not.

c

Those who rely on social media to find their news tend to be more polarized in their views. It is tempting to assume that social media is simply serving up a diet of content from the same two or three sources that their users have clicked on before, but it is more complicated than that. Readers who use social media and search engines tend to have a greater number of sources than people who go directly to news home pages, but they still have these polarized views.

This apparent contradiction is at least partially explained by the fact that once we look at the sources themselves, the political differences between them tend to be quite small. A large study of browsing habits in 2014 by the Pew Research Centre found that only 3% of the most extreme groups from the left or the right would ever visit sites that published views directly opposed to their own. A habitual foxnews.com or Newsmax reader might occasionally go to CBS News or the *Wall Street Journal*, but is extremely unlikely to give the *Guardian* or the *Huffington Post* websites a try. Equally, readers of the *Canary* or the *Morning Star* are not going to dabble with the *Spectator* or the *National Review*. The effect is stronger for opinion pieces than it is for hard news.

A

Even when social media forces people to be exposed to views opposed to their own, they are not likely to become more moderate.

Research has shown that oppositional media is likely to make polarized readers more entrenched, not less. The reader sees information coming from sources they believe to be untrustworthy, so they are actively inclined to disbelieve it, rather than take it at face value. The gap between tribes gets wider, rather than narrower.

B

Furthermore, as paywalls proliferate among quality news sites, a greater percentage of online news reading is on lower quality sites that are still free; these tend to be more extreme, as a way of attracting more traffic.

As online advertising, the income source of all of the major social networks, is increasingly used by campaigning groups, it is not only the content shared by peers that we should consider. Fortunes are spent on advertising on Facebook alone – $81 million between the Trump and Clinton campaigns in 2016, for example – and Facebook makes great play of advertisers' ability to show different messages to different people, in each case honed to their tastes through analysis of users' likes, comments and browser history. Surely this has to be more effective?

Public anxiety about the collection of data by big technology companies has been high, especially following allegations in the press of interference in political elections in Britain and the USA, centred on consulting company Cambridge Analytica.

A

B

Paywalls are digital subscription schemes implemented by websites. A reader might be able to access a few free pages to entice them into wanting to continue, but are required to pay a fee to access further content.

Cambridge Analytica were a political consulting firm who worked for the 2016 Trump campaign and the Leave side in the UK's 2017 EU referendum. Using illicitly gathered personal data they targeted swing voters in ways not covered by the existing laws on political advertising.

C

It is far from clear exactly how much influence Cambridge Analytica itself had on either the election of Donald Trump as president of the USA or Britain's referendum on remaining in the European Union, but it is true that they were able to amass personal details of not only the 270,000 people who unwittingly took a fun quiz called 'This Is Your Digital Life', but also 87 million of their Facebook friends, all without permission.

Is targeted advertising actually more effective? Only to a tiny extent. A few clicks in a thousand displays of an ad is all the difference it makes. In some campaigns – Brexit, for example, or the Trump/Clinton presidential race in close states such as Pennsylvania or Michigan – that might be all that is required. Small increments favouring one view over another can add up over a long time, but it is still personal sharing that appears to be making the bigger difference.

It is disquieting to learn that people know about you without your having given them the information. However, it is only in the improper use of such information – targeting with marketing messages for outcomes that will be against our interests but are designed to appeal to our personalities, for example, or depriving us of beneficial services such as health insurance based on spurious analysis – that it becomes dangerous. Public knowledge and scrutiny of the use of our data, such as Carole Cadwalladr's investigative work on Cambridge Analytica for the *Guardian*, is needed to be sure that it is used safely.

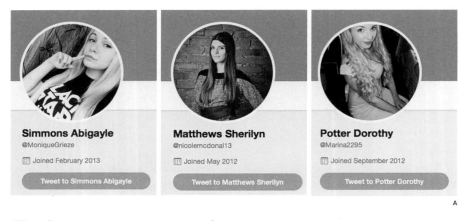

Simmons Abigayle
@MoniqueGrieze
Joined February 2013
Tweet to Simmons Abigayle

Matthews Sherilyn
@nicolemcdonal13
Joined May 2012
Tweet to Matthews Sherilyn

Potter Dorothy
@Marina2295
Joined September 2012
Tweet to Potter Dorothy

A

Fake personal accounts, usually referred to as bots, have become a problem for many social networks. Facebook deleted 3 billion such accounts between October 2018 and March 2019, as part of its ongoing routine operations against spam.

Away from news, loops can establish themselves in other forms of media. When a reader or a viewer finds something they are interested in, they are more likely to seek out more of the same, and to place more value on it. This can be a positive effect, such as communities of shared interest supporting each other, as in the rise of Mumsnet, for example. Or it can be a danger to our health, as in the anti-vaccination movement. Vaccination saves millions of needlessly early deaths, but some people resist it and are certain in their beliefs. A 2010 study in Germany found that there was an increase in anxiety over the safety of vaccines after just five minutes spent looking at an antivax website. People who are slightly wary search for facts, and find words that heighten their fears and people who compound them. People outside that community become opposition to be dismissed, and the positive attributes of community come to contribute to physical harm.

90

Todd Leal
@ToddLeal3

📅 Joined May 2017

Tweet to Todd Leal

James Reese
@JamesRe70999081

📅 Joined June 2017

Tweet to James Reese

Tom Mondy
@TomMondy

📅 Joined June 2017

Tweet to Tom Mondy

B

John Ruskin (1819–1900), the Victorian art critic and champion of the Pre-Raphaelites, is famous for allegedly being so turned off by his wife's pubic hair on their wedding night that their marriage was never consummated. Neither of them ever mentioned hair in post-break-up letters, but he did at times blame the difference between what he had expected her body to be like and how it actually appeared in the flesh for their abstinence.

Bots can be any automated processes run over the Internet. They started simply, scanning web pages for updates, for example, or sending spam emails. Now, more sophisticated bots can impersonate people on social media, holding very simple conversations and replying to key phrases.

Spam was used initially to describe unsolicited emails or newsgroup postings but it has come to mean any fraudulent or unwanted message, from automated marketed phone calls to direct postal advertising. The name derives from a Monty Python sketch of Vikings endlessly singing the word spam.

Mumsnet is a British online community for parents. Initially a place to discuss parenting methods and products, it has grown into a potent centre for political campaigning.

A Twitter automated fake accounts, or bots. These examples were given away by mismatching names and usernames, and accidentally reversing the order of first and second names.

B These bots gave themselves away by using the same picture more than once, and by using women's photographs matched with men's names. Not all bots are as easy to spot.

Art had been Ruskin's primary focus in life for many years and he must have seen hundreds, if not thousands, of paintings of nude women, but when it came to the real thing he was paralysed, and students of art history have cruelly chortled up their sleeves ever since. His problem is less unusual now.

Young people and children now have more access to pornography than ever before. Even the most debauched societies in history – 3rd-century BC Alexandria, for example, where a 50-metre-long (164 ft) gold phallus was paraded through the streets as part of the Dionysia festival, or late Pompeii with its erotic frescos and statues of satyrs surprising goats – have not been so steeped in graphic, detailed depictions of people having sex as any modern teenager with the most basic smartphone. Explicit photographs and videos of every kind of sexual act are now freely available at any moment to anyone with a pay-as-you-go Samsung.

A

B

Dionysia festival in ancient Greece, despite its gigantic symbols of sex and ivy-draped young women paraded around the town on carts, was fairly chaste compared to the later Roman version, Bacchanalia. This festival, according to historian Livy, was short on giant penises but long on sex and murder.

Paraphilia is abnormal sexual desire, especially when it involves dangerous, violent or extreme practices.

A   The all-women government-
funded hidden camera
hunting squad in Seoul,
South Korea, search for
cameras in public lavatories
and give out leaflets to raise
awareness of the country's
digital peeping problem.
B   South Korean women
protest against men
leaving cameras in private
areas and posting the
pictures to pornography
websites. The slogans read
'My life is not your porn'.
C   Pornographic models
Abella Danger, Honey Gold,
Kissa Sins and Jill Kassidy
pose at the 2018 AVN
Adult Entertainment Expo
in Las Vegas, Nevada,
attended by 15,000
industry professionals.

C

Across Europe, half of children between
the ages of 9 and 16 already have their
first phone. In the USA, half of children
under the age of 12 already have theirs.
In South Korea, more than 70% of
11-year-olds have one. Almost a quarter
of them have seen sexual images of
some kind, from naked photographs
to extreme paraphilic videos, by
the time they reach their teens.

Rising rates of impotence in young men have
been linked by campaigners to this trend. It is
certainly the case that impotence rates are on
the rise, but studies have shown very little or no
correlation between heavy pornography use and
failure to become erect with a partner. Some
even found the reverse to be the case, with some
people already experiencing erectile dysfunction
being helped by viewing sexual images.

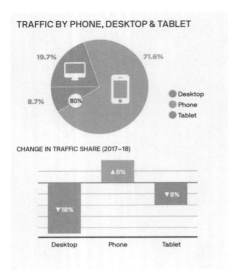

A

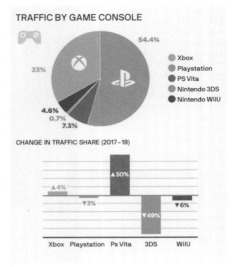

B

Defining sexual well-being as a male's ability to achieve an erection, however, is deeply misguided. Mental health problems associated strongly with viewing pornography include depression, anxiety, poor image of one's own body and sexual ability, and dysregulated mood. This has been found to be particularly the case in girls. Girls also report a far greater incidence of never seeking out pornography but of having been shown it involuntarily, a form of sexual assault that has mental health problems of its own and has become far more common with smartphone adoption.

In adult life, men who regularly view Internet pornography have been found to be less likely to be willing to use condoms, opening them and their partners up to the risk of sexually transmitted disease as well as unwanted pregnancy. They are also more likely to hold stronger stereotypical beliefs about gender, more likely to be distracted during sex by insecurities about their own bodies and sexual prowess, more likely to be disappointed by their partner's appearance if it does not resemble the models and actresses they see on screen and more likely to expect their partner's performance to resemble the fictional sex they watch.

It can be difficult to research the effects of sexual media on development. Experiments that remove all but one variable are almost impossible to achieve, and scientists cannot directly measure sexual aggression so have to rely on self-assessment and proxy results. All of this makes causation, rather than just correlation, hard to establish.

Evidence for the existence of true addiction – a need that persists even when causing evident harm, not just a habit or compulsion – to Internet pornography is extremely weak, however plainly some people have a compulsion to look, and look again. The theory that people are fed into a spiral of more and more extreme content when they become habitual users of porn is equally weakly supported by observation.

Internet pornography is banned in China and blocked by nationwide restrictions. In other countries such as South Korea, it is illegal but not blocked, and the law is rarely enforced. In a survey conducted in the USA, where it is entirely legal for consenting participants, 70% of women and 98% of men reported having viewed pornography online within the last six months.

A   Growth in the traffic to PornHub from phones, desktop computers and tablets, showing the greatest growth in mobile phone traffic.

B   Video games consoles are also a major growth area for pornography distribution and consumption.

C   PornHub offers analysis of its traffic data each year. Here it breaks down its most popular categories by country. PornHub employs the strategies of tech companies to collect and use data.

THE WORLD'S FAVOURITE CATEGORIES (2015)
The top PornHub Category in Different Parts of the World

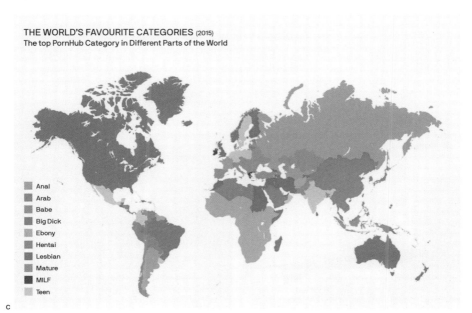

Anal
Arab
Babe
Big Dick
Ebony
Hentai
Lesbian
Mature
MILF
Teen

C

That a compulsion is not an addiction is not to say that it is not harmful. Research suggests that while non-aggressive men might not react to aggressive sexual portrayals, men who are already aggressive can take it as permission to behave differently with their partners.

Anecdotally, women have reported a change in sexual expectations to correspond to pornographic portrayals: the removal of all hair below the eyes, increased expectation of willingness to engage in oral and anal sex, and increased frequency of strangling and choking.

A   A technician removes amateur pornographic videos that have been posted online without the consent of the subject. So-called 'revenge porn' has seen a seven-fold increase in South Korea alone since 2016.

B   A man charged with posting 'revenge porn' online, which has been illegal in the UK since 2015.

C   Director Taro Kambe directs actress Yuri Oshikawa in a virtual reality pornographic film using a VR headset.

While there seems to be some positive outcomes of watching pornography – increased libido, increased confidence in discussing sex and more positive genital self–image, for example – Ruskin's experience of unfavourably comparing his new wife's body to those he had seen on canvas for many years is a familiar story in bedrooms around the world today. The Hook Model is deeply embedded in digital pornography consumption, making habitual compulsive use very widespread. Technology is in our bedrooms and it is far from clear that it is helping.

A

B

c

Internet gaming disorder (IGD) might be diagnosed if: the gamer experiences withdrawal symptoms when Internet gaming is removed; needs to spend increasing amounts of time Internet gaming; has unsuccessfully attempted to reduce Internet gaming; has lost interest in hobbies as a result of, and with the exception of, Internet gaming; continues with excessive use of Internet games despite knowledge of psychosocial problems; deceives family members and therapists regarding the amount of Internet gaming; uses Internet gaming to escape or relieve a negative mood; has lost a significant relationship, job or career opportunity because of participation in Internet games.

Viewing pornography is not by any means the only online activity that is possibly addictive. The *Diagnostic and Statistical Manual of Mental Disorders* (DSM) is the American Psychiatric Association's handbook for clinical practitioners, first published in 1952. It contains details, often in checklist form, of all recognized syndromes in the USA, and is used very widely to define mental health.

The latest edition, known as DSM-5 was published in 2013. It contains a call for research about the future inclusion of Internet gaming disorder (IGD), mooted as being rather like substance abuse disorder where the substance is not physically addictive, or like problematic gambling. It proposed nine possible criteria for diagnosing Internet gaming disorder.

A

There are undoubtedly people who suffer with such a compulsion. One study puts the figure at 5% of gamers, which would be more than 10 million people in the USA alone, and another 30 million in China. The question still remains, for many researchers, whether gaming itself is problematic.

Researchers in Germany in 2014 found that frequent *World of Warcraft* players have almost no increased neural activity in anticipation of a small reward, and even large rewards only elicited a similar level to that of non-players looking forward to something minor. They claim that IGD is closer to a reward deficiency syndrome, a dopamine deficiency in a particular part of the brain, causing the need for greater thrills in some people. Others, such as Orsolya Király and Zsolt Demetrovics in 2017, point out that gaming need not occur online to be addictive. Unlike gamblers or alcoholics, problematic gamers rarely hide their compulsion, so using deception as one of the nine criteria for diagnosing a gaming disorder is inappropriate. As gaming is itself a hobby, loss of interest in other hobbies is also not a useful criterion for pathology.

All of the studies looking at individuals who might be classed as Internet addicted have found that a very high proportion of them already have other disorders diagnosed, especially attention deficit hyperactivity disorder, depression, social phobia and, in males in particular, hostility. This makes identifying where the disorders stop and the Internet addiction starts very difficult, if not impossible.

If it were not the Xbox then it might well be solvents, sex, chocolate or gambling.

Usually the DSM gives a target score for diagnosing a condition. As a proposed condition, IGD has no target score as yet, but this checklist-led approach underlines the importance of making sure that all of the criteria are pulling their weight as part of a discrete treatable entity.

Dopamine is a chemical – $C_8 H_{11} NO_2$ – that naturally occurs in the brain and provides a medium by which signals are sent to the nerves. Higher levels of dopamine are associated with the reward function in the brain – the system responsible for both motivation and pleasure – and people with naturally lower levels can feel this loss as an emotional deficiency.

B

C

A

Seven of the nine criteria proposed for IGD are shared with those used to diagnose pathological gambling.

In-game mini-gambles are regulated differently around the world. China has banned them from direct sale, whereas Japan has classed them as 'prizes', and so brought them under existing gambling rules. A report by the British Gambling Commission on 'behaviour, awareness and attitudes' in 2017 noted the 'increasing convergence' between gambling and normal gaming.

Some online games use gambling mechanisms within their gameplay without classing themselves strictly as gambling, which can blur the lines between disorders even further. Loot boxes, for example, are objects available to buy within normal games that may or may not contain an artefact useful to gameplay. As these 'in-game mini-gambles' do not offer cash or material prizes, they are not always classed as gambling, are not regulated in the same way as poker or casino games, and are accessible to children in many countries.

B

The question is whether there are people who lean on gaming to the same extent as more traditional gambling, and in the same way, or whether gaming is being used as a mental crutch to help cope with pre-existing conditions. If the word 'addiction' is used for anything and everything that we crave, it explains nothing.

The answer appears to be that gaming is not used in the same way as traditional gambling. According to the best evidence we have, those who are counted as pathological gamers are likely to move on to other pastimes or compulsions within two years, without feeling pains of withdrawal. Many experience 'burnout', where they play a particular game in a way that appears obsessive for a period of time, then when its appeal wears off they enter a fallow period in which they play no games at all. This suggests that it is not gaming itself that is the source of the pathology, if there is truly pathological behaviour at all.

In this case, it appears, technology is the means by which we can know we are already sick, rather than the cause of the sickness itself.

Gaming, then, might not be an addictive activity in the same way that some drugs are, or even as gambling can be. But does it cause harm to the young people who are playing at war and murder in hyper-realistic environments when they come home from school?

A

A   Posters for *Call of Duty: Black Ops III*, an instalment of one of the biggest gaming franchises. Millions of dollars are spent each year on external triggers – advertising – for gamers.

B   Syrian children play games in the Atmeh refugee camp near the border with Turkey. Volunteers mended broken computers and set up generators so the children could play games while displaced.

C   A Lebanese man plays *Holy Defence*, a game developed by Hezbollah, in which the protagonist battles Isis fighters. The US military released *America's Army*, a combined video game and recruitment drive, in 2002.

B

C

Here is a medium, designed to entertain children, that is filled with blood, guns and death as the main driver of story-telling. Despite the existence of an age certification system, unsupervised children regularly take on the roles of killers, thieves, soldiers, reckless drivers and assassins.

Overall sales of violent games far outstrip those of other genres, such as sport or puzzles, even in these times of casual gaming on phones and an equal gender split in the gaming population. For many, it is their primary hobby. This, surely, must be affecting their minds, fostering aggressive tendencies and social isolation, and leading them away from other more wholesome pursuits, such as playing outdoors or reading.

A

As video games are such a wide-spread form of entertainment, it is not surprising that much research has been done into their effect on young (and older) minds. As with pornography, it is difficult to construct experiments that measure aggression or dysregulation directly without being stopped by the ethics committees, but longitudinal studies are widespread and they can establish correlation, if not causation.

Unlike pornography, violent games are unlikely to relate to any form of normal life without significant trauma. Most people will have some kind of sex life with a real partner, but in our largely peaceful society only a minority are involved in real violence and it still comes as a shock no matter how many levels of *Call of Duty* have been played.

The news, again, is that the link between aggression and heavy use of video games is extremely weak, especially once compounding factors such as family disruption, trauma and abuse are controlled for. Studies in the past, such as Craig Anderson and Brad Bushman's influential review in *Psychological Science* in 2001, have found a relationship between violent games and aggression, but more recently they have been found to be suffering from a terrible case of publication bias.

Pre-registration of trials can eliminate publication bias. Pre-registered studies looking at aggression and violent video games have not found that there is a link between the two.

A Staff members eat next to a man wearing a costume from *Fortnite* at a competitive gaming event.
B Fans watch Philadelphia Fusion play against London Spitfire in the *Overwatch* league in Brooklyn, New York.
C A teenage gamer playing *Fortnite* in the final of the EStars tournament in London, UK.

Publication bias is the tendency among researchers to only publish results that conform to a particular narrative, in this case that violent video games are associated with violent behaviour. If studies that confound that view are less likely to find a place in a journal, any review is likely to come to the same conclusion.

Pre-registration of trials is when researchers announce their methods before they begin, and commit to publication even if the results do not support their thesis.

B

C

Prosocial behaviour is that which is intended to benefit society or other individuals.

A   SuperBetter is an app that aims to apply some of the trappings of video games to improving its players everyday lives. Rewards are given for achieving goals such as exercise.

B   Three of the most popular games of all time: *Tetris*, *Candy Crush Saga* and *Bejeweled*. Recent studies have shown the benefit of playing games with high degrees of visual attention, such as these, immediately after traumatic events as they can reduce short-term post-traumatic stress disorder.

That is not, of course, to say that someone will not be aggressive after playing a game. There can be all sorts of reasons for that – social isolation, perhaps, or frustration at not being able to complete the game's goals or feelings of incompetence – but it does not appear to be the case that playing at shooting is one of them.

The developmental benefits of educational games are well documented. Educational games can help with setting goals, language and reading, number skills, concentration and, in multiplayer games, social skills.

A

Specialized games have been used to reinforce good habits in children who have to deal with medication, introduce safety information and aid in physical rehabilitation. Even notorious tech-sceptic Baroness Greenfield (b. 1950) gave her endorsement to a series of 'brain training' games called *MindFit* (although evidence for the effectiveness of those particular titles was limited, to say the least, and they are no longer available). There have been some attempts to measure the prosocial effects of benevolent games, which have seen glimmers of self-improvement through gaming, but they are not conclusive. It is very clear, though, that they do not do any harm.

So, if they are not addictive and they are not making us aggressive, can we say that video games are making us sick at all?

B

A   Students paying attention
    in an e-sports class
    in Lanxiang Technical
    School, Jinan, China.
    The class offers courses
    in video game techniques
    in order to attract students
    who aspire to careers
    in competititive gaming,
    tapping into a booming
    industry. E-sports
    leagues earned more
    than $1 billion wordwide
    in 2019 from tickets,
    merchandise, sponsorship
    and media rights.
B   Children relax in their
    playroom using their
    tablets and mobile
    devices. Estimates vary
    wildly on how much time
    children spend on screens,
    but it's clear that an hour
    or two is not unusual.

There is still the lack of exercise in a life spent gaming to consider, and the isolating effect of solitary games, as well as the fact that some gaming mechanisms do trigger anger, if not lasting aggression. There is mounting evidence that a dedication to video games over academic work can negatively affect grades, so might result in less achievement.

The widely mistrusted bogeymen of modern media – gaming, television, social media – are unlikely to be harmful in themselves, but they are part of compelling-by-design loops that exist entirely to draw their users back in over and over again, unthinkingly.

As Nir Eyal correctly points out in *Hooked*, this habit-forming method can be hugely beneficial. When we use it to encourage exercise, healthy eating, anger management or abstention from drugs or nicotine it can be life-saving. Problems arise when the habit former's goal itself is not a healthy one, or when the habit is unknowingly induced in an individual.

The loop can affect our conceptions and expectations of the world and our mental health, but the unthinking action itself is the greatest cause for concern. By definition, compelled behaviour is not free or deliberate. It might not meet up with the criteria for addiction, but it is a compulsion and a danger to individual agency.

Teenagers staying up late playing *Fortnite* to the detriment of their concentration at school are not addicted, but they are not making a free choice either. Someone who finds themselves skimming through screens full of Instagram pictures at work instead of getting on with what they need to do is not an addict, but they do not have full control of their life. They cannot just snap out of it any more than a smoker could snap out of a 20-a-day habit, or a troubled family can snap out of their relationship problems.

So what can they do?

4. Solutions for Restoring Health

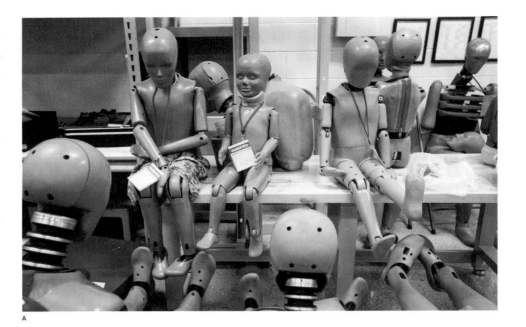

A

As technology is often a commercial product, the data we need to assess its safety is usually guarded as company secrets. The results of tests that revealed the link between smoking and cancer, or of thalidomide on foetal development, all existed in corporate reports for many years before they were made public. The users were not able to make informed decisions about their own safety during those years as they were not in possession of all of the facts.

Being harmed by unintended consquences is not inevitable. Some will always arise, but advance planning can reduce them. More diverse engineering teams would have avoided the danger to women posed by one-size-fits-all seat belts – women wearing seat belts are 73% more likely to die in a car crash than similarly protected men. Routine de-biasing of training data sets for artificial intelligence would eliminate racial discrimination learnt by recruitment filtering programs. A culture of sharing adverse or unexpected consequences and openness to user feedback, rather than trying to cover it up and hide it from the marketing team, would lead to faster improvements and less harm.

Technologists in the leading companies are very likely to have read Nir Eyal's *Hooked*, but are far less likely to have read Chellis Glendinning's *Notes Toward a Neo-Luddite Manifesto*. The people who have the least fear of the consequences of technology are in charge of making it, which results in a blasé attitude towards risk.

Many of the dangers to our health caused by personal technology could be avoided if there was greater awareness of them, but the companies that make handsets and apps are reluctant to acknowledge the dangers for fear of losing users. As a public health issue, this is entering the purview of the law.

Thalidomide was used to treat morning sickness in the late 1950s, but was found to cause severe birth defects and was much later taken off the market. Several attempts were made to reintroduce it in other treatments and under different names.

De-biasing in statistics is acknowledging the factors that might affect our decision making and allowing for them. Simple awareness of our biases has not been shown to be enough to disregard them, so they must be actively sought out and eliminated in order to achieve truly rational behaviour.

B

C

Government has always seen the enforcement of physical safety standards at work and in the home as part of its purpose. Our buildings are free of asbestos; our factories are risk assessed and dangerous machines cordoned off as a result. If modern technology poses a threat to mental well-being, that duty of care to citizens continues into the virtual, social world. Fulfilling this duty while not infringing individual rights of free expression or choice, or depressing an important part of the economy, is the line policy makers have to walk.

It is too simplistic to say that some technology is good for mental health and some bad. Sometimes, it is the very same characteristics that cause a positive reaction in some users and lead to anxiety, depression and self-harm in others. The ban hammer is an inappropriate weapon in the state's arsenal. Modern governments tend to shy away from blanket bans anyway, as they inhibit free trade. Much better to inform the consumer of the possible risks of their behaviour and let the market sort out the rest.

A

B

A   Representatives of Google, Californians for Consumer Privacy, Intel, DuckDuckGo and Mapbox are sworn in to a Senate Judiciary Committee hearing following broad support for greater regulations of American tech companies.
B   Elizabeth Warren, Democrat Senator for Massachusetts, is the face of a campaign to break up the biggest technology companies to reduce their ability to operate as monopolies.
C   The dominant market positions of companies such as Amazon, Google and Microsoft in various sectors of the technology industry.

GLOBAL MARKET SHARE BY COMPANY (2017)

Internet Search

- Google
- Other

Web Browsers

- Google
- Other

Cloud Hosting

- Amazon
- Microsoft
- Other

Desktop Operating Systems

- Apple
- Microsoft
- Other

Mobile Operating Systems

- Apple
- Google
- Other

Online Advertising Revenue

- Facebook
- Google
- Other

c

Companies that rely on secret intellectual property to form a habit in their users do not wish to explain their working methods. Only by being forced to do so, on pain of losing their right to operate in a country, can they be expected to comply. When it is clear how they exploit mechanisms that they have found to be compulsive, their users can make informed choices about whether they wish to continue to participate or not.

A **ban hammer** originally referred to a banning tool used by website administrators and moderators to block undesirable members from a site, normally achieved through blocking individual IP addresses. However the phrase is now used generally to mean the power to block or ban technology and online content.

Intellectual property refers to commercially valuable knowledge that is protected by law, such as patented inventions and copy-righted artistic works.

On a domestic level, parents and guardians have a new responsibility. As computer technology has the capacity to do harm as well as being a central pillar of our social and community lives, parents have to be willing to monitor and guide their children in their use of technology. Many of the worries about this technology are unfounded, but some underrated risks, such as the online radicalization of young men into terrorist groups or the effect of pornography viewing on partner expectations, are justified and backed by evidence.

A

It is essential that parents become knowledgeable about the effects of different systems, and how their own children are reacting to them. This means being prepared to monitor and discuss their online habits, just as they would take an interest in what they are eating or how much exercise they are getting. Devices such as the Netgear Nighthawk router can help parents monitor online activity in the home.

Many automated blocking software packages concentrate on shutting out pornography or barring access to certain apps, usually social networks. This is a very blunt approach to the problem, as porn filters can stymie access to legitimate sexual information that is useful to a developing teenager, and social networks can provide important social support. Artificial intelligence and deep learning techniques are making the filters more intelligent and nuanced, but the state of the art is still too unsophisticated to be relied upon completely. There is no substitute, as yet, for talking to your children.

The **Netgear Nighthawk** router has filters and monitoring built in, allowing complete control over online activity on any device connected to the household Wi-Fi. Apps, such as Mobicip and Watchover can also be used for monitoring your child's online activity.

Deep learning is a form of machine learning in which target data is analysed by a series of levels of computer scrutiny, each looking for a specialized area of focus. By refining analysis in this way the algorithm is able to extract more meaning than single-level scanning.

Digital detox involves putting down one's smartphone, tablet or laptop and spending time with friends and family and pausing to enjoy life. Its adherents report decreased stress levels and better sleep. According to a survey of British and US Internet users in 2018, 19% have gone on a full digital detox, and another 51% have attempted to lessen their time online.

When anxiety comes from the technological world, the solution often offered by everyone from educationalists to Sunday supplements is superficially attractive: the digital detox. There are hundreds of detox plans available, but they all concern themselves with three key areas: the use of technology while interacting with other people, the use of technology while also working on another task, and the unthinking use of technology to fill empty time. Relationships, focus and mindfulness.

Each plan recommends techniques to boost the three areas. These can include setting aside a day each month when the detoxer will use no tech at all, or a resolution to put devices aside when talking to children, or the practice of putting phones or laptops in slightly inaccessible places, so fetching them has to be a deliberate act rather than a habit.

B

A

There are certainly benefits to taking more time for self-care and relaxation, but digital detoxers depend on the idea that it is less healthy to use our screens, and more healthy to do something else instead.

Digital detoxers state that life in our physical surroundings is natural, and the antidote to life online. They maintain that people close to us are more important to us than people far away. This assumes that we are with the right people all the time and that our community exists in our proximate space, which might not be the case in our digital world.

We cannot say that digital detox improves any of the three criteria for a fulfilled life outlined in self-determination theory. Using willpower to stay away from technology that we find compelling is not autonomy or competence; it is purely an exercise in self-denial. Digital detox is cold turkey from something that can be genuinely beneficial, because of the fear of its harmful effect.

The keys to achieving self-determination in a digital landscape that seeks to funnel your choices into particular commercially valuable loops are understanding and awareness of the techniques being used on you. Once understood, the fear diminishes.

Self-care is not to be confused with self-indulgence. It is Audre Lorde, the black feminist activist, who is most responsible for the modern understanding of the term. In *A Burst of Light* (1988), a memoir of living with cancer, she wrote of self-care as self-preservation, an act of resistance against the oppressing forces of the world.

B

C

Knowing that an email alert is a trigger in the hook cycle, that clicking on a link within that alert is an action, and that the content you see when you have clicked the link has been designed as a variable reward, is a very different experience to being led through the process unthinkingly. Rather than having to avoid all forms of digital media because you cannot trust yourself with it, you are aware of the path you are following and the possibilities of your interactions with the software.

Technology companies also need to do more to assist users in deciding whether or not to use their websites, games or apps by labelling them appropriately. They should signal in advance any pornographic or violent content and alert users to the inclusion of in-game gambling. The safety of platforms for children could be clearly indicated using a traffic light system: for example, a green light might signal that your child will not meet strangers on the site, that it will not contain any in-game gambling and that it will switch itself off after an hour of continuous use; a red light would indicate that the platform is not recommended for use for children under the age of twelve.

A Punkt. mobile phones are designed to distract their owners as little as possible. They do not have a web browser or any other apps, and only show battery or signal icons if there is a problem.

B Samsung Marshmallow is a gamified app for teaching children the habit of controlling their own time spent on mobile devices. They set their own limits and are rewarded with icons and animations for self-discipline.

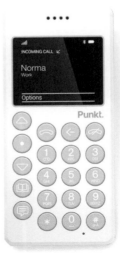

B

Considered objectively, you have options. Do you want to be an integrator or a segmentor? Which of your online and offline activities do you want to give highest precedence to? These questions are only answerable once you know how the triggers, internal and external, work and how they are applied by the companies you interact with.

> This knowledge is impossible without co-operation between tech companies, regulators and researchers, and that is unlikely to occur without the threat of legal sanctions. As with 19th-century factory owners, consumer pressure is not enough to change business practices. Only a digital equivalent of the 1833 Factory Act will make the social networking giants agree to be more open and responsible.

A habit, Eyal wrote, is an action taken without any conscious thought at all. Add conscious thought and analysis into the activities associated with technology, and freedom and self-determination are restored to the people who use it.

SMALL	MEDIUM	LARGE
	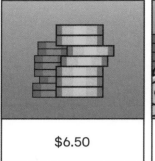	
$3	$6.50	$7

A

This mindfulness depends entirely on being sufficiently informed of the process. Until regulators force technology companies to be more open about their processes and to label their tech clearly in the manner in which food manufacturers are currently required by law to label their products, users will not be in a position to judge fully.

However, users can become more aware and exercise some degree of judgement.

It is difficult to jump into fully self-aware practice from a standing start, but progress can be made via a series of small steps. Many people have tried the pomodoro method of cutting off all Internet and alerts for 25-minute blocks of time during which they focus on one task. At the end of the period they go back to using the Internet until the next 25-minute break is scheduled.

This method can be effective, but it depends on abstinence rather than understanding, so should only be seen as an initial trial. In conjunction with this, you can be aware of the times and places you are using your devices. Setting aside times of the day you know to be problematic for you, such as active use of a blue screen in bed, for example, is something you can experiment with.

First, take a moment to look at the next marketing email or news bulletin you receive. Read it thoroughly and look for all of the possible actions you could take. There will be links directly to products, or stories you wish to read. Perhaps there are invitations to update your personal details in some way or interact with the company on a personal level. Even the unsubscribe link works as an action, increasing your chances of returning to the service on an internal trigger in future.

The **Pomodoro** technique is a time-management technique devised by Francesco Cirillo in 2009. He named a timed period of 25 minutes a 'pomodoro' after the tomato-shaped kitchen timer he used. Between each pomodoro, users take a break of three to four minutes, with a longer break of 15 to 20 minutes after the fourth.

A The highest-priced in-game virtual goods are often examples of 'decoy pricing': items that only exist to make the mid-priced offerings seem like more of a bargain.

B Amazon held a patent on its 1-click purchasing system, reducing the amount of conscious thought required to make a purchase, which expired in 2017.

B

 Add to Cart

or 1-Click Checkout

 Buy now with 1-Click®

A

Compare them with the invitations on their previous email. See how they differ, offering you variable rewards for your clicking action. Try to predict what will happen when you click on each one, then decide on the outcome you find most favourable, and click.

When you arrive on the page, look at the options you are offered. There will be content you want to see – the reward – and also options for giving a little more of yourself to the service. That might be the option to buy something, personalize the pages you would like to see or share the fact that you are here with your social network. All of these things have intrinsic value for the company, but they are also designed to make you feel that you have invested something of yourself with them, in order to make it more likely that you will return.

Real world time is a phrase used to refer to time spent with people in your physical surroundings, in distinction to time spent communicating electronically with those who are not geographically present.

Your awareness of the hook cycle makes it less likely to embed itself into an unthinking habit, and makes you more able to judge the value of your actions each time you perform them. As many social and online content companies provide valuable services, you are unlikely to want to be completely abstinent from them.

A   Unplugged Coding is a teaching programme that aims to kindle greater understanding of coding in children through the use of tangible objects such as paper and markers. Role-playing, analogies and other offline activities help the students to grasp the underlying logic of computer code without requiring them to learn the syntax of particular programming languages.

B   A Russian expat living in Australia stays in touch with his community in his home country over email. Lonesome cowboys are entirely confined to the pre-Internet age.

You will be able to rank them against other things in your life, though, and give them appropriate amounts of your time. Less attention to Twitter, more to your partner. Less to WeChat, more to your textbooks.

Time spent completely offline can be useful, but mostly in order to give you some perspective on how much you miss the services you are spending time with. What the digital detoxes call 'real world time' is not intrinsically more valuable simply because it happens in the space around your body. The ability to live in the future, to avoid future shock, consists of being able to deliberately commit your attention to the things that matter to your life, which relies on dispassionately judging your own actions.

You can be online, you can be offline, as long as you know where you are.

B

Conclusion

Progress that sticks rather than technological change that will be forgotten, unused, comes from solving existing problems rather than working towards an ideal. The solutions bring their own problems, and the technologists, engineers, social scientists and architects set about trying to solve them anew. In the past, it has been disease control and water supply, now it has shifted more towards the psychological and the social.

Limited preparation for the worldwide use of inventions has meant that many problems have not been foreseen. Insufficiently diverse development teams have not taken into account the variety of people who will use the things they develop, and this has meant that large numbers of people have been excluded or endangered by technological progress. Greater communication and equality of opportunity are lessening this effect, but it still exists in large measure.

A

A   Senator Robert Menedez introduces legislation in the US to encourage education in state schools on Internet safety in 2009. In 2018, 83% of UK adults reported that they have concerns about harms for children online.

B   A Malaysian woman blurs the boundary between her office and the rest of the world, taking work into a solitary meal in a restaurant.

The bleeding-edge technology of the previous generation is the boring status quo of the now. Last century's impossible-to-anticipate bugs are the everyday frustrations of people at large, and the market for their solutions makes demands on creative scientists.

Our current technology has particularly brought us problems of mental health, physical isolation combined with social feedback that reinforces our prejudices and sources of anxiety and depression, rather than challenging them.

A

B

A   Signs warn of health risks at the largest electronic scrap yard in Agbogbloshie, a district in Ghana's capital, Accra.

B   The Agbogbloshie scrap yard deals with many types of electronic waste including fridges, televisions and computers. The recycling process that recovers copper and other valuable metals from the scrap releases toxic smoke into the surrounding atmosphere.

C   Expectant parents can now monitor foetal growth on an app linked to ultrasound scan data, and view the foetus through virtual reality glasses as a virtual object, or opt for a 3D printout.

D   Visible Body makes 3D anatomical illustrations that can be experienced in real situations through the use of augmented reality – the overlaying of computer images on surrounding physical space.

Our global supply chains still include exposure to dangerous materials away from the consumer, masking the physical problems that our technologies still cause to the extent that it appears that they do not cause any. This makes it difficult to persuade a large number of people of looming environmental catastrophe.

The problems caused by existing technology become the pressing questions to be answered by the next generation of inventors. In their solving, they will cause problems of their own. Meanwhile, public awareness and political pressure can work to minimize the effects of our current issues.

Life expectancy and infant mortality, the two strongest lines on the graph of physical well-being, have never been in a better state than they are now. Affluent, well-supported people who look after their own health can expect to live three times as long as their Neolithic counterparts. Children are nine times less likely to die in their first year than they were 100 years ago, and their mothers are more than 100 times less likely to die in childbirth.

Centuries of health and safety innovation and regulation have resulted in workplaces that are extremely unlikely to cause severe harm in well-ordered countries, and our ingenuity continues to make work safer in all areas of the world. Pressure from governments and, to a lesser extent, consumers to take danger out of their products ensures that companies work to make all parts of the supply chain safe, although there is a lot still to be done.

Life expectancy varies around the world, but it is rising everywhere. In Japan and Singapore, Europe and the USA people can expect to reach the age of 85. In China, the average is 76. Central Africa has the worst outlook. In Chad, you are likely to live for only 51 years. Child mortality plays a large part in these averages, but average survival for all ages is going up, too.

Infant mortality refers to the proportion of children who die in their first year against the total number of live births.

C

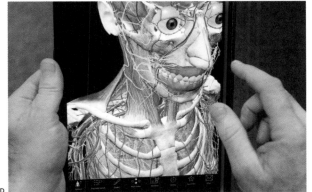

D

A

As our life expectancy increases, our habits and personal lives become more important in determining our level of well-being. Our diets, prosperity and attitudes to exercise take over as determinants of our healthy life expectancy, rather than the machines we have built and live with. This is a long way from saying our technology no longer makes us sick.

Despite many scare stories and understandable but unfounded fears, our mobile phones and computers are not making us physically ill in the same way that technology of the past was harmful. We have RSI and eye strain, but we do not lose limbs or lung function. The newest technologies we use every day are exerting control over our mental well-being in different ways, and we have yet to adapt to many of them.

Always-on work stress, destructive virtual communities, frequent use of pornography from an early age and unconscious adoption of compulsive habits take away our freedom and reduce our feelings of competence and agency, essential for contentment and fulfilment.

Mental well-being has been the first victim
of our new paradigm, just as in previous eras
we fought cholera, leprosy and malnutrition.

We will not give up our new
machines because of the clear
benefits they bring, in the same
way that all progress of the
past involved accepting
disadvantages in order to solve
pressing problems. They are
a cure for loneliness, a guide
to the discovery of new interests
and knowledge, a boost for
productivity and vital tools
for development of new and
even more amazing technologies
of the future that we will adopt
just as eagerly.

B

A

The scientific, experimental method and modern project management techniques have brought about a time of technological wonders that would have been unimaginable only a century ago. The science fiction of previous eras paints a picture of flying machines and cumbersome robots, and all but the most prescient writers completely missed the coming revolution in mobile communications and connected media and data. While they have huge advantages, they also impact on our health.

New changes follow the same old pattern, and people work to solve the problems inadvertently caused by the last set of solutions. Better experimental and analytical tools mean that the pace of change increases all the time, allowing faster fixes for our current problems and the more rapid introduction of new ones.

B

A   One hundred and
    ten years after Louis
    Bleriot first flew
    across the English
    Channel, Frank Zapata
    takes off to make the
    same journey on a
    jet-powered 'flyboard'.
    This attempt failed
    but he succeeded
    a week later.
B   The futuristic decor of
    the Experience Centre
    in Bangalore, India,
    lures customers in
    to look at the newly-
    launched OnePlus
    7 and OnePlus 7 Pro
    mobile phones.

Our lawmakers will have to help us if we are to be fully aware of the changes around us, and we will have to apply pressure to them to provide that help. Once we have the tools, it is up to us to use them if we value our mental well-being as well as communication, convenience, speed, anti-isolationism and progress. Then we can really say that the technology is there for us, not the other way round, and that our health is as important as the spread of the new.

Further Reading

Aaronson, Scott, *Quantum Computing since Democritus* (Cambridge: Cambridge University Press, 2013)

Baldry, Chris et al, *The Meaning of Work in the New Economy* (London: Macmillan, 2007)

Ball, James, *Post-Truth: How Bullshit Conquered the World* (London: Biteback, 2017)

Bijker, Wiebe E., Hughes, Thomas P. and Pinch, Trevor (eds.), *The Social Construction of Technological Systems: New Directions in the Sociology and History of Technology* (Cambridge, MA: MIT Press, 1987)

Brautigan, Richard, *All Watched Over by Machines of Loving Grace* (San Francisco, CA: Communication Company, 1967)

Chivers, Tom, *The AI Does Not Hate You* (London: Weidenfeld & Nicholson, 2019)

Colvile, Robert, *The Great Acceleration: How the World is Getting Faster, Faster* (London: Bloomsbury Academic; New York, NY: Bloomsbury USA, 2016)

Criado Perez, Caroline, *Invisible Women: Exposing Data Bias in a World Designed for Men* (London: Chatto & Windus; New York, NY: Harry N. Abrams, 2019)

Deci, Edward L. and Flaste, Richard, *Why We Do What We Do: Understanding Self-Motivation* (New York, NY; London: Penguin, 1996)

Etchells, Pete, *Lost in a Good Game* (London: Icon Books, 2019)

Eyal, Nir, *Hooked: How to Build Habit-forming Products* (New York, NY: Portfolio Penguin, 2014)

Foucault, Michel, *Discipline and Punish* (New York, NY: Pantheon Books, 1977)

Fry, Hannah, *Hello World: How to be Human in the Age of the Machine* (London: Doubleday; New York, NY: W. W. Norton & Company, 2018)

Gates, Bill, *The Road Ahead* (New York, NY; London: Penguin, 1995)

Glendinning, Chellis, *My Name is Chellis and I'm in Recovery from Western Civilization* (Boulder, CO: Shambhala, 1994)

Goldacre, Ben, *I Think You'll Find It's a Bit More Complicated Than That* (London: Fourth Estate, 2014)

Greenfield, Susan, *Mind Change* (London: Ebury Digital, 2014)

Guernsey, Lisa, *Screen Time: How Electronic Media – from Baby Videos to Educational Software – Affects your Young Child* (New York, NY: Basic Books, 2007)

Harkaway, Nick, *The Blind Giant: How to Survive in the Digital Age* (London: John Murray, 2013)

Harkness, Timandra, *Big Data: Does Size Matter?* (London: Bloomsbury Sigma, 2016)

Jones, Martin, *Feast: Why Humans Share Food* (Oxford; New York, NY: Oxford University Press, 2007)

Kahneman, Daniel, *Thinking: Fast and Slow* (New York, NY: Farrar, Straus and Giroux, 2011)

Kardaras, Nicholas, *Glow Kids: How Screen Addiction Is Hijacking Our Kids – and How to Break the Trance* (New York, NY: St Martin's Press, 2016)

Kuhn, Thomas, *The Structure of Scientific Revolutions* (Chicago, IL: University of Chicago Press, 1962)

Kurzweil, Ray, *The Age of Spiritual Machines* (New York, NY: Viking Press; London: Phoenix, 1999)

Kurzweil, Ray, *The Singularity is Near: When Humans Transcend Biology* (New York, NY: Penguin, 2005)

Lanier, Jaron, *You Are Not a Gadget: A Manifesto* (New York, NY: Knopf, 2010)

Levine, Rick et al, *The Cluetrain Manifesto: The End of Business as Usual* (Cambridge, MA: Perseus Books; London: ft.com, 2000)

Lorde, Audre, *A Burst of Light: Essays* (Ithaca, NY: Firebrand Books; London: Sheba, 1988)

Markoff, John, *What the Dormouse Said: How the Sixties Counterculture Shaped the Personal Computer Industry* (New York, NY; London: Penguin, 2006)

Negroponte, Nicholas, *Being Digital* (New York, NY: Vintage Books, 1995)

Nelson, Ted, *Computer Lib/ Dream Machines* (Redmond, WA: Tempus Books of Microsoft Press, 1987)

Ries, Eric, *The Lean Startup: How Constant Innovation Creates Radically Successful Businesses* (New York, NY: Crown Business; London: Portfolio Penguin, 2011)

Schumacher, E. F., *Small is Beautiful* (New York, NY: Harper Row; London: Blond & Briggs, 1973)

Stross, Charles and Doctorow, Cory, *The Rapture of The Nerds* (New York, NY: Tor Books, 2012)

Toffler, Alvin, *Future Shock* (New York, NY: Random House, 1970)

Walker, Matthew, *Why We Sleep: The New Science of Sleep and Dreams* (New York, NY: Scribner, 2017)

Weizenbaum, Joseph, *Computer Power and Human Reason: From Judgment to Calculation* (San Francisco, CA: W. H. Freeman & Co., 1976)

Picture Credits

Every effort has been made to locate and credit copyright holders of the material reproduced in this book. The author and publisher apologize for any omissions or errors, which can be corrected in future editions.

a = above, b = below,
c = centre, l = left, r = right

2 © Burt Glinn/Magnum Photos
4–5 Kyodo News/Getty Images
6–7 © Martin Parr/Magnum Photos
8 PjrStudio/Alamy Stock Photo
9a imageBROKER/Alamy Stock Photo
9b Roberto Esposti/Alamy Stock Photo
10 Wellcome Collection, London
11 Library of Congress, Washington, DC
12 Amoret Tanner/Alamy Stock Photo
13 George Tiemann and Company, New York, NY, 1899
14 Stephen Lam/Getty Images
15a NurPhoto/Corbis via Getty Images
15b Ulrich Baumgarten/Getty Images
16 Atlantic Monthly, July 1945
17a Gail Oskin/AP/Shutterstock
17b Pam Berry/The Boston Globe via Getty Images
18 Charles McQuillan/Getty Images
19 David Tran/Alamy Stock Photo
20–1 Nutexzles
22 Thierry Zoccolan/AFP/Getty Images
23 Michel Porro/Getty Images
24l PCJones/Alamy Stock Photo
24r Stephen Barnes/Technology/Alamy Stock Photo
25 Anton Novoderezhkin/TASS via Getty Images
26–7 Stefan Wermuth/AFP/Getty Images
28 Savvas Zannettou, Tristan Caulfield, Jeremy Blackburn, Emiliano De Cristofaro, Michael Sirivianos, Gianluca Stringhini, Guillermo Suarez-Tangil
29al durantelallera
29br clker
29bl Asbestos (Sam Fentress)
30a Brendan Smialowski/AFP/Getty Images
30b Greg Baker/AFP/Getty Images
31 Stephen J. Dubner/Getty Images
32l Fairfax Media via Getty Images
32r Kim Komenich/The LIFE Images Collection via Getty Images
33 Craig F. Walker/The Denver Post
34l Gadgethacks.com
34c iphonehomescreen.tumblr.com
34r Doni Bobes/Twitter
35 Our World In Data
36 Woohae Cho/Bloomberg via Getty Images
37 © Jonas Bendiksen/Magnum Photos
38 Matt Blyth/Getty Images
39 Ed Gold, www.edgold.co.uk
40 Alain Pitton/NurPhoto via Getty Images
41 Giulia Marchi/Bloomberg via Getty Images
42 Reuters/Vincent Kessler
43a David Paul Morris/Bloomberg via Getty Images
43b David Becker/Getty Images
44–5 Mint Images/Shutterstock
46 Andrey Rudakov/Bloomberg via Getty Images
47 Ed Lefkowicz/VWPics/Alamy Stock Photo
48 Kevin Frayer/Getty Images
49 Miguel Candela/SOPA Images/LightRocket via Getty Images
50 Kevin Frayer/Getty Images
51 Reuters/Devjyot Ghoshal
52a Hans Klaus Techt/AFP/Getty Images
52b John Macdougall/AFP/Getty Images
53 United States Patent and Trademark Office
54l Frank Lingwood/Alamy Stock Photo
54r Alexandra Jursova
56 blueblockglasses.com
57 Reuters/Kim Kyung-Hoon
58 Anthony Wallace/AFP/Getty Images
59 Qilai Shen/Bloomberg via Getty Images
60 Christophe Simon/AFP/Getty Images
61 David Chang/EPA-EFE/Shutterstock
62 Michael Robinson Chavez/The Washington Post via Getty Images
63 Fred Dufour/AFP/Getty Images
64a STR/AFP/Getty Images
64b Sanjit Das/Bloomberg via Getty Images
65 Homer Sykes/Alamy Stock Photo

Index

Acknowledgments:
The author would like to thank the patiently
exacting Jane Laing and Isabel Jessop and their
colleagues Tristan de Lancey and Phoebe Lindsley
at Thames & Hudson, Tom Chivers of course,
Nir Eyal, Pete Etchells and Amy Orben for sharing
their vast knowledge and wisdom, Emma Barnett
and Shane Richmond for all those years, Alec Lom
for telling him he should do it in the first place,
Nick Harkaway for unexpected answers and
Lindsay, Holly and Murray Douglas for everything.

MIX
Paper from
responsible sources
FSC® C112556

First published in the United Kingdom in 2020
by Thames & Hudson Ltd, 181A High Holborn,
London WC1V 7QX

Is Technology Making Us Sick? © 2020
Thames & Hudson Ltd, London

Text © 2020 Ian Douglas
General Editor: Matthew Taylor

For image copyright information, see pp. 138–139

British Library Cataloguing-in-Publication Data
A catalogue record for this book is available
from the British Library

ISBN 978-0-500-29531-1

Printed and bound in in Slovenia by
DZS-Grafik d.o.o.

To find out about all our publications,
please visit **www.thamesandhudson.com**.
There you can subscribe to our e-newsletter,
browse or download our current catalogue,
and buy any titles that are in print.